TIME TO THINK AGAIN!

*Christian Belief in Today's
Age of Increasing Confusion*

Barry L. Callen

EMETH PRESS
www.emethpress.com

Time to Think Again: Christian Belief In Today's Age of Increasing Confusion

Copyright © 2025 Barry L. Callen
Printed in the United States of America on acid-free paper

All rights reserved. No part of this book may be reproduced, or stored in a retrieval system or transmitted in any form or by any means, electronic, mechan-ical, photocopying, recording, scanning or otherwise, except as permitted by the 1976 United States Copyright Act, or with the prior written permission of Emeth Press. Requests for permission should be addressed to: Emeth Press, P. O. Box 533, Jackson, Georgia 30233. http://www.emethpress.com.

Library of Congress Cataloging-in-Publication Data

Names: Callen, Barry L., author.
Title: Time to think again : Christian belief in today's age of increasing confusion / Barry L. Callen.
Description: Jackson, Georgia : Emeth Press, [2024] | Includes bibliographical references. | Summary: "Barry Callen calls for a carefully considered faith that entails an enriched reason that is beyond reason. He pleads for contemporary Christians to develop a perspective on how to think and believe again in the highly secularized West. He argues that it is time in the postmodern world for Christianity to show that it reflects a rational foundation in real history and an emotional intelligence that is transrational (not irrational). He argues that it is important to spell out the implications of postmodernism for the Christian gospel so that the new generations can understand"-- Provided by publisher.
Identifiers: LCCN 2024050305 (print) | LCCN 2024050306 (ebook) | ISBN 9781609472108 (paperback) | ISBN 9781609472115 (kindle edition)
Subjects: LCSH: Faith. | Christian life. | Postmodernism--Religious aspects--Christianity.
Classification: LCC BV4637 .C295 2024 (print) | LCC BV4637 (ebook) | DDC
  234/.23--dc23/eng/20241213
LC record available at https://lccn.loc.gov/2024050305
LC ebook record available at https://lccn.loc.gov/2024050306

Contents

	Pages
Introduction……………………………………………..	v

Chapters:

1. Out of Balance……………………………………........	1
2. Contrasts in Thinking …………………………........	11
3. The Next Generations? …………………………......	19
4. Mystery Guides Mastery …………..…………….....	29
5. Outlasting the Deviations ……………………........	37
6. Being Caught Between ………………………..........	47
7. Wisdom Involves a "Quad" ……………………....	57
8. The Authority of Spiritual Experience ……….......	67
9. Having a Solid Place to Stand ……………….........	81
10. In the Company of the Committed …………….....	93
11. Christ-Centered Christian Universities ……….....	103
12. One Faith Among Many? ……………………..........	113
13. Think Again Before Winter Comes …………........	127

Introduction

Man obviously is made for thinking. Therein lies all his dignity and merit; and his whole duty is to think *as he ought*. Now the order of thought is to begin with ourselves and with our Author and end.
–Blaise Pascal, *Pensée* 620

I attempt here to help us think again, *and as we ought*. I pick up where I left off, the endings of two of my works of Christian theology. This, then, is a Christian theological primer for our present time. Here's where I left off.

"The God who knows us fully is known by us feebly. The Father is the ground of all being, the Son is the Father's expressed Word of saving love, and the Spirit is the ongoing presence who guides us into all truth as it is in Jesus Christ."

"We all are travelers, brothers and sisters on a continuing faith journey. We don't begin to arrive until we realize that it's been the loving and suffering God all the while having been moving toward us."[1]

Why start again and begin with these thoughts? Today we believers are being forced us to think as deeply and clearly as possible. It's a time of great confusion and possibility. The air is filled with "spiritual" affirmers, deniers, detractors, proclaimers, experimenters, and escape artists. Our secularized world doesn't believe, and yet it does, or at least it wants to and doesn't know the way. Do we Christians? If we do, can we communicate clearly?

Our time is confused about what to believe, whether to believe at all, and certainly about how to answer either of these critical questions. It takes turns going in multiple directions and then in none. It's open to being "spiritual" but likely not "religious" in any conventional sense. The whole Western world now stands in this awkward transitional place, caught between the working of the mind and the longing of the soul, and lacking workable definitions of either.

Current analysts of "the truth" are trying to champion or somehow combine two contrasting ways of human knowing. One is the "enlightenment" (modernism) that proudly elevates human reason and science, and the other is a "post-modernism" that's skeptical of the potential of human reasoning and very aware of its mixed results to date. Thinkers now are exploring "spiritual" alternatives in reaction to the recent dominance of human reason. Theirs is an awkward position that appreciates reason without any longer bowing a knee to its obvious and often self-serving frailties.

Beginning Caution

Where is God in all this confusion? Everywhere or nowhere? By historic definition, God *is the truth* and, biblically speaking, God has shown a definite desire for that truth to be known. The problem is that we humans are troublesome students.

The early thirteenth century has been described much like today, full of ambitious people craving for aggrandizement, causing a mad scramble for honor and fame. That sounds like yesterday's news broadcast, only with a little less traffic and more leprosy back then. The worst diseases of yesterday now are being unearthed in the melting permafrost.

Many Christian believers have reacted to the present confusion in too aggressive a manner. Some have become ultra-conservative, highly defensive Pharisees again needing considerable correction from Jesus. Such Christians are risking the rocky path of being all head with little heart and no humility. We too easily revert to being brittle thinkers about mysterious and majestic matters. We are tempted to be hyper-enlightenment people, too quick to claim our ability to reason out and know for sure things that have baffled others for centuries.

Good reason should prompt mere humans to proceed humbly, willing by faith to believe, although short of any arrogance that exceeds our best thinking capacities. A carefully considered faith, I will argue, involves an *enriched reason*, not *un*reason but something beyond mere reason. Such is urgently needed today before winter comes.

Enriched reason is more easily stated than defined. Definition is one goal of these pages. A preface to that definition might be this. The key to human wholeness is the pursuit of the truth of God through Jesus Christ. All other paths to truth are fragmentary at best and their outcomes sterile and finally unsatisfying.

Announced Blaise Pascal in his *Pensée 188*, "Reason's last step is the recognition that there are an infinite number of things which are beyond it. It is merely feeble if it does not go as far as to realize that." How important and yet difficult it is to see life not just in the context of a particular time and historical situation, but in the context of eternity. Human reason finally must bow at the feet of Jesus who is eternity come to be with us!

Ancient and Modern

A prominent American journalist, a Western "rationalist," recently was in Istanbul, the ancient city bridging Europe and Asia. He was trying to figure out the Sufi brand of Islam and how it might speak to his own religious uncertainties in these modern times.[2] Local Islamic guides explained to him that Sufi is a "mysticism" within the Islamic family, one particularly concerned with the inner experiences more than the outer practices of religion. The need is to find the spiritual bridge from West and East, between rational mind and spiritual soul.

This journalist, the model of today's postmodernity, was told that he needed more moral meditating and less scientific theorizing. This would get him away from analyzing religious issues to learning by focus more on the "holistic perception" of reality, one colored with more affection, inspiration, and mercy. Their Sufi advice was, "Just surrender. This we call *islam*, submission." These mystics in Turkey were suggesting that God is found less in the theoretical hereafter and more in the rich quietness of the deep now. The Eastern world of Christianity has leaned in this general direction for centuries.

Our journalist friend heard this advice with appreciation and skeptical caution. Then he traveled more widely and tested Buddhism in Kathmandu. Here the "religion of no religion" conceives of "God" as the ideal state of the human mind, affirmed in order to survive the surrounding suffering by a calculated faith of denial. Wisdom doesn't lie in any "metaphysical" affirmation. Wrote Lama

Yeshe, "The experience of an atom of honey on your tongue is much more powerful than years of listening to explanations of how sweet it is."

Such wings of Islam and Buddhism are two ancient communities of mystical faith that claim to have found "God" everywhere and nowhere, except deep inside one's own meditating being. Such ancient claim to wisdom sounds quite "post-modern." Does it have anything to say to the contemporary Christian community? Is there essential truth in either Turkey or Nepal, or only more dangerous diversion? Should we be Westerners or Easterners in our current faith journeys, right-brained or left-brained, or somehow those who seek to straddle the two?

Again, what is "enriched reason." Unfortunately, definition is difficult. Our times are calling us to try to define and maybe embrace the result if it offers actual enrichment of the faith once delivered to the original Christian saints. We moderns hunger to know. It's time to think again.

Now we seek to know by reaching for our smartphones and swiping and clicking with our fingers. All knowledge seems in that magic little box, from ancient Egypt to quantum physics. But grabbing at a fact needed at the moment isn't enough. We still hunger, need more, swipe again and again, maybe eventually realizing that what we really need is a wisdom not captured in the magic box. We're flooded with information and starving for wisdom.

Consider a homerun in today's professional baseball. We instantly are informed of the ball's speed off the bat, the precise trajectory as it flies away, and how far it goes almost to the inch. What the data can't tell us, however, is which team to root for or why we should go to the game in the first place. Should I have visited the nursing home instead where an uncle is dying, the one I should be forgiving or encouraging as death approaches?

Wisdom is something other than having the right computer files and statistical spreadsheets. It's discovering thoughtfully a preferred way of being in the world in light of human origin and destiny. Wisdom is less a *what* and more a *how*, and especially a *why*. Christian faith goes even further. It comes down to a *Who*. If that is the case, our human reason finds its needed enrichment well beyond itself.

Looking Ahead

The following chapters attempt to provide perspective on where we are as contemporary Christians trying to think and believe in the now highly secularized West. How did we get here, where ought we to go, how might we manage to get there, and why should we even bother? Admittedly, everything to follow will be a bit tentative. That's the nature of our faith journey as Christian pilgrims. Wisdom isn't easy, only essential. It's very reasonable while also being quite *trans*-rational.

At best, we humans will know only in part. Even when following Jesus, the master teacher and central subject of his own teaching, we will have just begun the quest. I believe God helps our unbelief and guides our journey to meaningful ends. Christianity has the advantage of being more than a religious tradition that on the one hand theorizes about the beyond or on the other hand tries to suspend the brain and just meditate about things deep within. It claims by faith, well-founded in real history, that the Beyond *has come to us* to orient our theorizing and give substance to our meditating!

We Christians launch our theological quest by believing that divine initiative has given us opportunity to *taste the drop of honey*, not just analyze the possibilities of its theoretical presence and goodness. The sweetness of creation has come to have a face, Jesus, and in him offers us personal friendship. We must think again and need not do it alone. The Spirit of Jesus thinks with us and even for us.

Doing theology as Christians is to be thoughtfully open to the Spirit who guides us to the Son, who faithfully represents the Father. After our best thinking takes us to that foundational place, and we must think again, we also must remember that spiritual things are finally best tasted rather than merely analyzed.

Chapter One

Out of Balance

Paradox lies at the heart of the Christian understanding of human existence. In theology, "orthodoxy" is faithful paradoxical belief. Jesus is human and divine, fully, equally. The church is the body of Christ while a collection of human believers often confessing their unbelief. "Heresy" often isn't falsehood but having a key theological paradox out of balance. When all questions are fully answered, something is wrong. God's revelation isn't intended to answer in advance every question we humans raise. It's to introduce us to the One who is *the Answer*. It's hard to keep all this in balance!

The Western journalist mentioned in the Introduction is Eric Weiner. Even though born Jewish, the Old Testament God hasn't been his own, not really. No "god" clearly was or is absolute for him. On the one hand, he has come to think that an atheist is just "too cooly confident." It's very hard to announce a universal negative. Who of us is smart enough to know for sure that there is no God?

Agnostics, on the other hand, claim more humbly to be without any sure knowledge of divinity. That's a more respectable stance, although Weiner fears that such people don't care as much as they don't know. He personally is closer to the belief of a typical postmodern person. "I am spiritual but not religious."

That stance seems to be today's common crowd. It appreciates the great spiritual seekers of the past and present while tending to stay away from any of their specific belief systems. I'll enjoy the froth while leaving behind the drink itself.

Weiner refers to himself as a "confusionist," deeply confused about religion but not with the smug uncertainty of the agnostic or the unfounded arrogance of the atheist. They both seem seriously out of balance. His better balance is a blurry somewhere-between position. He has a spiritual longing and hopefulness without anywhere specific to hang his hat. This he assumes is true of many people today just like him. Christian theology must address them understandably.

"We're not exactly clear what we're not clear about," Weiner admits. "We confusionists throw our arms skyward and shout that we don't know what to believe, or whether maybe we do. Even so, we're open to the unexpected, and we believe, even hope that there is more to life than meets the eye. Beyond that, we are simply and utterly confused."

As a foreign correspondent for National Public Radio, Weiner's experience living in Jerusalem did little to rehabilitate in his mind the God of the Hebrew-Christian tradition. "I saw firsthand what was done in his name, and it wasn't pretty."[3] The public today easily sees the downsides of Christian church life. Beyond that, we fear, most believers are too busy with their rampant consumerism to care much about Christianity's current doctrines and institutions. They consume even their religion, going where the fine the most satisfaction, whatever label is over the door or creeds are on the books.

Addressing the "Confusionists"

Things in the church are out of balance and need adjusting. Should the ministerial preparation of today's Christian leaders focus on human reason and formal education or nurturing spiritual gifts from God designed for perceiving truth inwardly and serving humanity visibly? Must we choose between these options? Should we leave our minds on the coatracks of the churches or take them to the pews to think seriously about the faith in today's world? Do we have anything helpful to say to the "confusionists"?

Do humans know and serve best with their thoughts or hearts? Do we live in a world of the rational or the spiritual? Is science the answer or a tool taking us to our destruction? Is the church overly dependent on human reason and its institutionalizations? Is it failing to affirm what's beyond reason's reach? We live in a rational *and* a spiritual world. It's always both, and the careful balancing of them is especially required of today's Christian community. The Spirit-inspired genius of the Wesleyan faith tradition of Christianity suggests an effective balance of faith and reason.

Theological inquiry and social interaction easily deteriorate into being like a drunk man getting on a horse. He falls off one side only to get up and fall off the other. These extremes are very current. In a time of exploding knowledge of a "factual" sort, the easy option is to let reason take its course or to let unreasoned faith become the counterforce behind which we hide unreasonably.

Today's Christian community is under heavy stress. It has spawned ultra-modernists who rush to biblical "inerrancy" and are quick to judge other believers harshly. There also is the opposite, the ultra-progressives who seem to champion nearly anything new as a fresh and welcome frontier of the faith, judging harshly all believers stuck in their stale traditionalisms. Both are hurtfully defensive, trying to save the faith from its many detractors by its own brand of extremism. Most of these believers, of whichever sort, are well-meaning and loved brothers and sisters who are choosing an easy but hardly ideal path to protect and proclaim the faith of Jesus Christ today.

The synthesis of faith and reason, held in tension by the Holy Spirit and the wisdom of church tradition, can yield both intellectual and spiritual integrity. Charles Wesley pled properly, "Let us unite the two so long divided, knowledge and vital piety." Our heavily rational recent time (modernity) is now being challenged by a (post-modernity) countering of the supposed capacity of human reason to grasp the depths of life and the heights of truth. There is a undoing of the rational dominance without bringing clarity to any viable alternative.

We must think again, learning how to appreciate the paradoxes of Christian truth without giving up the essentials that lie behind the paradoxes. This will take patience, maturity, and a willingness to live partly in the "cloud of unknowing."[4] Sometimes the acceptance of not knowing is the first big step in coming to actually know. Such stepping into the yet unknown seems required of the Christian thinker in today's post-modern environment. This is an important but hard thing.

There's fresh hope for the Christian community in this "un-reasoning." There also is much danger. The faith is highly rational in that it makes sense in light of all we know. It also is trans-rational (not *irrational*) in that it stretches by faith in a reasonable manner beyond what reason can otherwise reach. Christianity fits both modernity and post-modernity when each is at its best.

Rather than this being a time for the Christian faith community to despair, it's a time to rethink the available means of human knowing. It's the challenge of knowing how best to read the Bible as God intends and discover there the motive and means of church mission.

Today is a time when the mind-set of "modernism" still hangs on with its rationalism while "post-modernism" has taken hold with its challenges and uncertainties. We face a sharp critique of the arrogance of rationalism combined with a yet undefined awareness of what is more than the rational.

Suspicious of the claims of atheism and even of agnosticism, the new generations of post-moderns are now open to filling life's void with something beyond and above and deeper than the capacities and agendas of only human reasoning power. But with what? That's where the confusion and current challenge come in.

Where does this leave Christianity with its dual claims of being a faith tradition that is both very reasonable and also one stretching far beyond the capacities of human reason? Answers are needed and quickly. Whatever Christians put forward as an answer, it must be accompanied by *experience* and *performance*, the twin language of post-moderns. Little hope exists for a church that proclaims loudly but doesn't back it up with life change and mission action.

The faith claims of the Jesus people must be embodied in real and believable persons and communities that are demonstrating their relevance in today's often tragic social settings. Public perception of Christians must come to exceed that of Eric Weiner's negative observations in Jerusalem and his judgment of agnostics who appear to not care as much as they claim to not know.

Do we who claim to follow Jesus really believe? Do we really care? Do we take seriously the teachings of Jesus *and* the power of his Spirit? Are we willing to *be* church or satisfied to just *play* church? We'd better be or likely we are to get nowhere in today's confusionist setting. Want to be a Christian theologian today? It will be quite a task!

An Awakening Humanity

Humanity is awakening slowly from the long night of "modernity" and entering the confusing light of some new "postmodernity." It's a move from the dominance of the reasoning of science toward something more "spiritual" and unquantifiable. This is a big challenge with new opportunities for the Christian community.

Science and philosophy are being pressed to jettison their sometimes grandiose claims for themselves. There must be less technical and yet marvelous dimensions of reality. This new trend might be only the popular byproduct of a self-obsessed culture. It also might be a heightened awareness that there is more than meets the eye, more than the material in this world.

With "artificial intelligence" surging around us, isn't reality now whatever some technician designs it to be? The new mindset is more a "laid-back pluralism," the acceptance of a diversity of truth perceptions and lifestyles that resists any one being thought absolute for everyone. Maybe there are no truths, only truth perceptions that prevail within given communities of faith at given times and places.

Can Jesus people speak meaningfully in such an environment? We must accept the task of deciphering the implications of this post-modernism, rethinking and embodying our faith in ways that new generations can understand and appreciate. "Under the banner of the cross, we must boldly go where no one has gone before."[5]

Was *Star Trek* right about space being the final frontier? Is there such a thing as "final"? What frontiers of faith need crossed today? How can this be done without the integrity of the faith being compromised? How can soul and mind both be guided in a mutually beneficial way?

We have plenty of tools available for fresh thinking. They include advanced scientific capabilities, huge computers and telescopes, the internet, and a "cloud" bulging with oceans of stored data. But are these adequate to accomplish the task? Can they look beyond technical bits and pieces to the mysteries of life and the longings of the soul resistant to being satisfied with only a deluge of data?

Humans are more than minds. Theology is more than carefully crafted creeds. Peace and justice will not emerge from any amount of knowledge. The more we know the more we humans seem inclined to misuse the knowledge in service of our greed. The spirit of the human must be nurtured, honored, and somehow re-formed. Wisdom lies somewhere beyond our computer files, professional titles, and statistical analyses. It has "fallen." How can it stand again? In the church, wisdom is more than the best-honored traditions and well-honed practices. It also, maybe primarily, lies with actual new life in Jesus Christ.

Christian faith has the capacity and now the need for the functions of mind *and* spirit. Too often it has wandered far to one side or the other, following the shifting cultures of its many human settings. Christians now need to *re-think* and *re-experience* the meanings and implications of its multiple ways of knowing and defining truth.

Let's give fresh attention to the Spirit of God calling to our human spirits, sometimes through the mind and often otherwise. Mystery is calling to mystery, deep to deep. This world is rational, yes, but sadly irrational and by faith also trans-rational. Our souls can feed on knowledge while withering and even dying if not nourished by more. The young of today are looking for a more responsible, authentic, and *God-alive* church that both makes sense and fills the spiritual void.

For Christians, proper thinking necessarily begins with a major assumption, a delicate complexity. God exists as *Trinity*, the great Three-in-one, the eternal Person (Father) who has reached (Son) and is reaching in love to all persons (Spirit). While perceptions of God are partial, God wants to be known and has provided at least an adequacy of knowledge. This adequacy has a strong relational dimension, knowing the Person *in person*.

By "Trinity" we admit to belief that stretches the mind into the world of the spirit. We are expressing awareness of the one God who is not a solitary and unapproachable being. God is a communion of love overflowing with life itself. The Trinity is a doctrinal symbol in frail human language and imagery pointing to a three-fold relationality. The being of God is Father-Son-Spirit. Shared life lies at the heart of the universe. Mutual relationship is the paradigm of God's intention for all personal, social, and religious human life. The Father has stooped our way in the Son and is very much with us in the Spirit.

Hope in Our Present Time

What follows is an exploration of the dimensions and implications of such divine reality. They are largely compatible with the longings and instincts of post-modern people. They are beyond rational pretenses and the limits of human language. They speak to the desperation of broken communities and lives in search of meaning. They offer the potential of restorative love and meaningful evangelism.

My theological work once was described as "on the progressive side of the middle." I like that characterization. I suppose I'm something of a "recovering fundamentalist."[6] I said this to the Wesleyan Theological Society in 2023:

> Regarding religious truth, it's human to know and not know for sure. Although the biblical message is fixed, how best to conceive and apply it is fluid. Balance is critical between the fixed and the fluid. Christian "experience" can be a common centering for the global Christian community with all its diversity. Such spiritual experience, to be truly Christian, requires a limited and carefully chosen *fixed*, what is absolutely core Christian doctrine, while it allows for a considerable range of *fluidity*. The experience of new life in the Spirit is a unifying reality that forms and enables the church everywhere.

The challenge now before us Christians is not to be washed away in a flood of the fluid. True spirituality is not a mere mist of nothingness.[7] The quest is for the essentials, the fixed, allowing much of the rest to travel fluidly as the Spirit of God may direct. My attempted role in this shifting time of confusion between modernity and post-modernity is to be a middle-man. I wish to hold to the good of yesterday while being open to the fresh and needed good of today.

The charge given to the 2024 graduating class of Asbury Theological Seminary included this. "We live in a reductionistic world with little patience for serious reflection. The whole glorious Christian gospel has been reduced to simplistic phrases, bumper stickers, a Twitter feed or Instagram or TikTok post. This trivialization of information, a reductionism of all things sacred, and the shockingly short attention span now confront us as bearers of the eternal gospel in the 21st century. But, in any age, and whatever the challenges, the gospel is still good news!"

This charge went on to insist that the success of Christian ministry today will be in sharp contrast to what Julius Caesar wrote to the Roman Senate in 46 B.C. after a stunning military victory. *"Veni, Vidi, Vici"* –I came, I saw, I conquered bragged Caesar. Christian success will not happen now "through an exercise of power, but through humility, patience, and love." The Christian motto must be *Veni, Vidi, Amavi*, I came, I saw, I *loved.*"

God is still at work. Christian thinking must be surrounded and infused by our loving. When it is, and when we don't know exactly what to think or say, the Spirit of God promises to fill our minds and mouths with the inspiration of heaven (Ps 81:10; Rom 8:26). Such filling depends on an important assumption key to this book. Christian truth does not change but times do, making it necessary on occasion to rethink some of faith's language and life expressions.

We must think again, reconsider our views of the Christian faith, even think again *about the limited value of thinking*. Thinking may not be the only or at least the most important task being faced. God is prepared to fill our lives with fresh inspiration for proper understandings and applications of our faith in a changing time. The most important task is to actually *be in touch* with God who is reaching to be in touch with us and today's world.

We must encounter or be encountered by the Divine in community experience (church), personal transformation (sanctification), and sacrificial living (mission). This will require an altered way of viewing and reading the Bible, a shift from a strictly "objective" mindset to one that is more subjective. This less rational view of the Christian life is very biblical and urgently necessary if we believers are to impact the post-modern world for Jesus Christ.

What follows attempts to explain the fresh thinking that needs done, thinking even about the limited value of thinking alone. To a lingering degree, the need is still "modernist," and to a significant degree also post-modernist. Put otherwise,

Reason is an excellent tool for solving problems but offers little guidance in identifying which problems we should solve and why. Reason makes a wonderful servant but a poor master. Reason cannot account for those moments in life that bewilder the intellect yet utterly quiet the heart.[8]

We believers and Christian theologians must not fear the transrational. We must account for and profit from those moments that bewilder, the ones that quiet the heart. Senior Christian churchman David L. McKenna specialized in integrating the apparent tensions of Christian knowing.[9] It's time to listen to leaders like him. If you haven't thought carefully, be careful about believing boldly. If you have reached very logical conclusions, don't fail to submit them to the speaking and cleansing of the Spirit of God. We need to embrace the complexity of faith's knowing. We also need to be enriched by this complexity without becoming paralyzed "confusionists" in the process.

Chapter Two

Contrasts in Thinking

> Faith does not cease being active as it undertakes the process of rigorous thinking. One need not disavow the gifts of intellect in giving thought to their Giver. –Thomas C. Oden
>
> It is the vocation of the Christian in every generation to out-think all opposition. –David Elton Trueblood

It's time to think again *about thinking* on behalf of the Christian faith! The stakes are high and everyone is involved. We humans are created with minds and reasoning power. What then is the role of reasoning when it comes to religious believing and witnessing? This question is freshly urgent in our "postmodern" time. Whatever it limits, now is hardly the time to abandon reason.

Is reasoning pre-eminent in the human knowing and theology framing processes? Is it subservient, with faith setting the scene of perceived reality and reason just ordering the perceptions for public consumption? There is an inevitable complexity to the processes of thinking, believing, "knowing," and theology establishing. All these require a careful balancing act. Today there is disagreement about how much to balance with what. Regardless, we must not disavow the divine gift of reason or abandon the challenge of out-thinking all opposition to our faith's legitimacy.

The Christian community should realize that the best witness to the faith today will have to be more than talking about our religious thoughts and establishing institutions built around them. The best faith witness will have to be evidenced clearly in transformed lives that incarnate and actively share the best of our thinking. Religious logic brought to public attention must be supplemented with actual *living* that goes well beyond what the public hears. It wants to *see*.

Gracious deeds must attend all Christian words and concepts. If they don't, credibility of even the best faith reasoning will fail. The marketplace is full of religious claims and well-funded logical arguments for nearly everything imaginable. Believers must act out credibly what they have thought out carefully. We must feel deeply what we analyze technically. To be Christian, life's actions must look very much like Jesus. They can if the activity of the mind is fused with the actual life of the Spirit.

Atheism is Too Irrational

Denying the very existence of God is popular these days. The public has a taste for "deconstruction." It also has a fresh taste for more than the void of raw rationalism and the blanket denial of the spiritual realm. Atheism is too simple an answer for the complex reality we humans are and face. It's an illogical sidetrack on the human quest for ultimate truth. It too easily denies much more than it has the capacity to judge. None of us is capable of declaring a universal "No!" Deconstruction has its limits. There must be more to life and destiny than a meaningless present and an empty future.

There are two general approaches to thinking about human existence. One is the *materialist* and the other the *religious*. The first assumes that matter and space and people just happen to be. Nobody knows why because there apparently is no why. We humans may seem to know that we ought to act in certain ways, but for no particular reason other than that we just do. There is no grounding to the *ought*. Everything came into being by some fluke that produced creatures like ourselves who just happen to be able to think about a "plan" that unfortunately doesn't exist.

Maybe something hit our sun and produced the planets we know. By pure chance the chemicals necessary for life occurred on one of these planets and some of the matter on this particular one we now call Earth came alive and eventually developed into things like us. There's no rationale for it, just the odd fact, the accidental event. The irony is that we humans are capable and even driven to reason about the wholly irrational. We insist on sensing something behind the senseless. By ironic instinct, we believers try hard to focus on nothing—and then joyously say we've found it!

The other option to thoughts about life's realities is the religious view. Behind all this existence and amazing development of thinking and morally conscious beings does indeed necessarily stand a creating and planning "being," one who is conscious, has purposes, initiates, prefers for us one life path over others, and has built that preference into our very beings. This "God" created the universe, intending that there be creatures like ourselves who are deeply loved and have free wills to choose what is divinely intended.

Humans are created in the image of God and thus able to perceive, think about, and decide for or against the "oughts" built in. This set of abilities makes possible our experiencing and expressing love and goodness. It also makes "evil" possible, the word "live" spelled backwards, our ability and often choice to live backwards as never intended.

Our world today seems to specialize in the backwards direction, violating love, defying God's natural law, and even denying God's existence altogether. We are said to be accidental realities, responsible to nothing but ourselves, thinking in a void, living for the immediate. Still, there is a longing for meaningful joy and rich community and moral guidance that would bring deep satisfaction. Such confusion of assumptions and desires and frustrations define our times.

In the Christian version of the religious view of reality, one man once appeared suddenly in the little town of Bethlehem in ancient Israel. Soon he was talking like he was God with us and claiming to forgive our "sins," our violations of what instinctively we know to be right and yet choose to do anyway. About this man Jesus, there is one thing we cannot say logically. It's that "I'm ready to accept Jesus as obviously a great moral teacher, but I don't accept his claim to be God with us." That's illogical, unacceptable even if popular thinking.

Why is it improper to say one thing and deny the other? Because a mere man who said the sort of things Jesus said would not be a great moral teacher. He either would be amazingly correct in his claims or a lunatic, like a man claiming to be a poached egg. There is no reasonable middle ground. In fact, what this man Jesus *did* argues strongly for the legitimacy of what he was saying about himself, God with us and for us.

Especially shocking about the doings of Jesus is the fact that somehow he survived a brutal death and keeps giving evidence of *still being alive* and with us lost humans! No bones have been discovered, only millions upon millions of disciples claiming that he is very much alive within them. Opponents have failed for centuries to downplay this reality. This argues for his being correct about everything he taught and did, including his life, death, and resurrection. Somehow Jesus still manages to heal our broken relationships with the creating God. Once healed, we are motivated and gifted to set about healing the world around us by his Spirit.

How do we choose today between the *materialist* and *religious* options for understanding all of reality? Science alone is not capable of making the decision. Some faith will be required for either direction. Keep in mind that choosing the materialist view requires a very large leap of faith. Choosing the Jesus perspective isn't an automatic, but it's highly satisfying and fully credible when all things are considered.

Especially convincing are the first disciples of Jesus who abandoned him after the crucifixion. They were gripped with a crippling fear that they would be found out as once his friends. Then, following his resurrection, the same disciples became bold new people putting their lives on the line to witness on his behalf. They refused to back off no matter what the threat, even martyrdom.

According to C. S. Lewis, believing this whole story about Jesus is high-level thinking, "mere Christianity." It sets atheism aside as too irrational to be entertained by seriously thinking people. Isn't it now time to think the Lewis way again? It does require some faith, yes, but so does any alternative, and the Jesus way calls only for a rational faith that fits all the facts we know and fulfills the life for which we long.

Ages Come and Go

Naming ages of human history is an arbitrary process of broad generalizations. Even so, the process does give helpful perspective. The "Dark Ages" from about the fifth to fourteenth centuries after Christ, especially in Europe, was the long period that followed the collapse of the Roman Empire. It featured the dominance of authoritarian religion and a relative dearth of cultural creativity.

Then came the Age of Renaissance, a period from the fourteenth to the seventeenth centuries, launched especially in Italy. It was marked by a revival of classical Greek and Roman influence, enriched by a flowering of the arts and literature and the beginnings of modern science.

During the eighteenth century there arose the Age of Enlightenment or Reason when many philosophers felt that traditional Christian dogma didn't fit well with the new "enlightened" (rational/scientific) view of things. This Age stressed the supposed supremacy of human reason for determining truth and achieving human social progress. Such thinking had significant impact on the young United States, particularly through the famous pamphlets of Thomas Paine. He attacked the Christian church for being corrupt and too institutionalized, out of touch with the time and future as he envisioned it.

Paine's proposed alternative? "Deism," an aberration of classic Christianity. It affirmed the existence of God but denied that God has had miraculous dealings with the universe after its creation. The supremacy of human reason had been allowed to take over. God was reduced to a clockmaker who designed the complex machine and then released it to function on its own by natural laws and preset scientific principles. Reality, then, is best known by thoughtful scientific studies of the workings and results of such "natural law." This supremacy of human reason became the accepted means for discovering true reality and manipulating it for human good.

"Ages" of human thinking keep shifting. In more recent generations, "modern" people have been dazzled by major scientific advances that have radically altered life for better--and worse. While human reason has been exercised extensively, the Age of Reason now has largely ended. Why? Because in the twenty-first century reality is being perceived as more complex than its physical appearances and natural workings. Despite all the past debunking, religion remains very much alive in many human societies, however "advanced" they claim to be.

Values, mystery, and the world of the "spirit" appear real and crucial for human satisfaction and even survival. It's increasingly clear that even the most advanced science isn't the absolute truth source, and certainly no guarantee of the highest human good. We still are choosing to live backwards (evil being "live" in reverse), now with more dangerous tools in our hands. Everything can't be discovered by careful reasoning alone, even with massive computer programs, international space stations, and telescopes of any size.

There are worlds within and beyond the physical. Mere human reasoning isn't capable of determining whether all this vast network of worlds began with some big bang or a quiet word from God creating from nothing. God may exist outside and inside time, still very much involved in creation's workings and in full control of the ultimate future. We can't be fully sure except by faith. Even so, we are sure that the alternatives to the assumption of God seem increasingly unlikely and require large amounts of faith.

"Artificial intelligence" is a dramatic new technology surging around us, making it harder than ever to determine what's real. Is an object what it appears to be or something machine generated? A picture is no longer worth more than a thousand words since a photo can be altered in a thousand ways.

With so much shifting and uncertainty, what "age" of human history is now upon us humans? The "modern" is yielding to the "postmodern." While what that means is still being clarified, it's growing alongside the remaining culture of "modernity" yet influencing most people in the Western world.

Freedom now is being understood as an inherent right of the human self apart from "God" or anything else preventing the exercise of independent life choices. What Benjamin Franklin thought about personal success is still valued highly in the United States. America is said to be glorious because it hopes to provide everyone the opportunity to get ahead on her or his own initiative and terms, being self-made individuals.

The grand goal is human freedom without constraints and conditions. This leads to a culture of consumerism, the drive to fulfill every want and even whim dictated by nothing other than one's private preferences, which are nurtured and manipulated by a rampant blaze of advertising. Religion often is resisted because it's seen as designed to control freedom and shut down uninhibited life.

Self-centeredness is now pictured as almost natural, normal, desirable. Advertising encourages going after things we don't need but have been convinced we can't live happily without. Focus is kept on ourselves, our pleasure, possessions, income, and status. Even some popular forms of "successful" church life now have joined this narcissistic parade, announcing that God wants believers to be "first-class" in this life, making God look real and generous. Support the church and God will bless one richly with health, wealth, and eternal life.

Thinking this way builds crowds, fills offering plates, and dilutes the faith into a virtual byproduct of secular culture. It's time to think again! We must outthink the opposition and start again listening to Jesus who says that giving up our self-centered lives is the only way to find true life!

Chapter Three

The Next Generations?

The church of Jesus must regain its vitality and capacity to nurture souls in the face of the illusions, pretensions, and eroding values of today's new and quite secular culture. Christian citizenship is to be transferred in baptism from one dominion to another as we become *resident aliens* in this world.

Let's dare to embrace without apology the "scandal" that some of us believers supposedly are. We need to boldly pursue the quest for love's knowledge and love's language. We are to be known as a people of experiential religion. A core part of the Christian tradition is a passion for God.[10]

Reviewing the trail of past human ages is of some value with its broad perspective, but not fully adequate for serving the generations now here and still to come. The Christian faith always must adjust to the current context, but without changing its very nature. It needs to adapt its expressions and applications for necessary relevance. The "mere Christianity" of C. S. Lewis remains the message of Jesus. Nevertheless, refreshing elements of its exterior must be found for the sake of the 2020s and not the 1940s.

We Christians are, after all, "resident aliens,"[11] a colony of heaven seeking to gain a foothold in this lost and fallen world. Are we ready for such a challenge? It will involve picking up a cross and humbly following the divine Master. We can be "citizens of high heaven" (Phi 3:20) with minds that begin to think like the mind of Jesus (Phi 2:5). It's surely time to think like that for the sake of new generations of believers and their witness in this world of today and tomorrow. Such rethinking is the task of Christian theology.

Two prominent Christians awoke a few years ago and realized that few people believed anymore in the "old time" Christian faith. It used to be that young parents, college students, auto mechanics, and others believed that one almost becomes a Christian just by breathing the air and drinking the water in the hospitable environment of Christendom America. That day is gone.

The church used to be the only real show in town. Church, home, and state joined to form a national consortium working together to instill at least "Christian values" in new generations. Now things are very different. Only when the church dares to believe and embody the scandalous, the Jesus-centered tradition will it truly be the body of Christ that can survive with integrity and transform such a new world into the image of Jesus.[12]

Going to New Places

The popular TV series *Star Trek: The Next Generation* completed its final season in 1994. Its creators had discovered that the world of their audience was in the midst of a major paradigm shift. Modernity was giving birth to some sort of "post-modernity." Modernism with its *objectivity* was shifting to a post-modernism with its elevated *subjectivity*. This major cultural change may rival the scale of innovations that marked the birth of modernity out of the decay of the Middle Ages.

This TV series became a popular reflection—and perhaps a molder—of the fresh worldview of today's emerging generations. The character Spock had been the ideal modernist, heavily rational, keeping emotion and speculation in check and solving urgent problems by his hyper-rational expertise. Episodes began with, "These are the voyages of the starship Enterprise. Its continuing mission—to explore strange new worlds, to seek out new life and new civilizations, to boldly go where no one has gone before." Such going now would require more than Spock onboard.

The amazing technological machine that was the Enterprise would get them to these new worlds, and Spock would keep trying to solve anything that went wrong enroute. The goal of these voyages was not to colonize new discoveries but to learn from them, peacefully if possible. New "peoples" found elsewhere may know truth previously unknown to earth-bound humans. Europeans had come to the Americas to conquer and plunder and Christianize. Now we humans are on our way elsewhere, and much more humbly, with both our big machines and our still unmet human hungers.

Postmodernism signifies this quest to move beyond modernism and its Spocks. It involves an increased subjectivity supplanting a fixed objectivity. Many historians place the birth of the "modern" era at the dawn of the Renaissance and then the Enlightenment. These centuries elevated humankind to the center of reality. Francis Bacon envisioned humans exercising power over nature by means of the discovery of nature's secrets. Building on the Renaissance, the Enlightenment elevated the individual self to the center of truth and value. These were essentially anti-Christian shifts and much of the church accommodated, institutionalized, rotted in its own apparent success..

René Descartes defined the human person as an autonomous rational subject. Isaac Newton pictured the physical world as a machine with operations that could be discerned and controlled by the human mind. The modern human was considered an autonomous rational being encountering Newton's mechanistic world and explaining and manipulating it as desired.

The world perceived as "modern" is the one into which I was born, but increasingly it's the "post-modern" world in which you and I now live. It has its great challenges, but also its great opportunities. The new spiritual sensitivities are calling out. Jesus still is the answer. When enough of modernism gets deconstructed, maybe something new, even something very old, may emerge again as surprisingly viable, highly desirable, and ultimately true. We will, however, have to think again about many things, including our view of the Bible itself.

People in the past thought that we humans develop documents like the Bible to provide known meaning that helps others make sense of their life experiences. All societies were presumed to possess or were stretching to discover the same thing, the one fixed reality behind our world and lives. More recently, the world has shifted to waves of questioning "deconstructionists." It's now more typically assumed that there may be multiple worlds and a wide range of perspectives on truth that in some sense are really true.

Philosophers now are insisting that the meaning of our human reasoning and written texts is dependent on the perspective of the individual writers and readers. The same thing can have multiple meanings. According to postmodernism, reality can be different for each self who encounters it. There is no one meaning or singular truth, no meta-narrative behind the world's origin and functioning.[13] Old "orthodoxies" need disassembled and rebuilt by the perceptions of each person, society, and faith community. Our perceptions of truth are shaped by our primary life communities. Each is a truth-maker and none can claim superiority over the others. Christian theologians today must face and counter this pluralistic perception.

Ages of human thinking about the very value of human thinking come and go. We "Western" people in the twenty-first century tend to think we are in an age verging on "unreason." That is, there is no "objective" knowledge equally true for all people. This leads to a radical individualism at odds with any religious faith that leans on the Bible, which is assumed to provide access to knowledge that is objective, ultimate, and applicable to all.

If God is, much of what God's being implies may yet lie beyond our human comprehension. Can faith still claim that God has reached us within an essential understanding of basic divine things that are real and real for all people? It likely can within church walls. What about outside those walls?

This challenge now is considerable. Christian thought today throbs with elements and instincts of post-modernity. This offers real hope. It also holds to a singular perception of ultimate reality that contradicts today's pluralism. This presents a major challenge that demands us to think again about how to present the one Christ to the world's many.

The Age of Enriched Reason

Humans have done much thinking about the value of their own thinking. Now the church of Jesus needs to do the same about its theological thinking in the midst of a radical post-modern mentality. When it does, the best thoughts are likely to tell us that there is so much more to the fullness of reality than our human reason can reach dependably.

Let's be clear about one thing. It's not that the creation of God is unreasonable. It's that it's *supra-reasonable*. Reality is what we can see, touch, test, count, and measure; and yet *it is more*, apparently much more! The New Testament knew that "faith is the assurance of things hoped for, the conviction of things *not seen*" (Heb 11:1). As the Jews knew long ago, reality is not individualistic as modernists presumed, but corporate, relational, created by a God of covenant relationship (Trinity) and relationship building (church).

It's time for the church to enter the Age of *Enriched Reason*. In light of all that's presumably "known" by science, this new faith age needs to feature a well-reasoned faith that reaches humbly beyond the capability of mere human reason. Faith will know confidently, although not arrogantly, about realities yet unseen. This elevated knowing will not be because of superior reasoning but necessarily by the gracious provision of God. Faith, when joined by divine grace, can approach the ultimate of the unseen.

If reason is the prose of reality, it's time to add faith dimension of poetry to our reality perceptions. Of course, Christian faith can be an escape from present reality in favor of an invisible reality presumed better but unreal. It also can and should be an immersion into present reality that is enabled to glimpse the higher reality. How? By actively receiving and representing the transforming impulses of what already has come in Jesus Christ, and eventually will arrive in its fullness in the return of Christ.

If the world now has entered a post-modern age, the biggest things of life no longer are clear to the general public. It marvels at science and then despairs at its uses that damage our environment and extend the destructiveness of our constant wars. We are caught between high potential and very low performance on behalf of the common good. We are beginning to realize that reality has depths greater than the reach of our minds, and yet we don't want to function mindlessly. Are all perceptions of the "beyond" humanly created and likely wrong?

Thinking globally with its dramatic diversity today, who knows what's right and for whom and beyond the present moment? Who's qualified to judge? Heard often is, "If it fits me and feels right, then it's right, at least for me and those like me." Is this chaotic situation of radical pluralism all there is? Subjectivism is claiming dominance, although "objectivism" is stubborn and won't go away. Where is the Christian church community in all this? Where should it be?

The answers are multiple and hardly stable. It's time for the church to think again about even its thinking. Fundamentalisms are rampant despite the individualistic plurality of our time. They are defensive reactions. A similar situation can be seen in New Testament times. Does everything change or nothing? Jesus said he had not come to throw out the old but to refresh it in more life-giving ways. That's still his intent. Dare we be his "radical" and refreshing people for our time?

Alternate Ways of Thinking

We spoke above of two ways of understanding all reality. There also are two general ways of human thinking.[14] One assumes that there are objective truths applicable to all people at all times. These truths must be learned and taught in order to properly order and direct our families and societies. The large truths are givens, even revelations if one believes in God. This is *deductive* thinking, working from an assumed premise of existing truth to current and necessary expressions and implementations of that truth.

What always is right is what should be thought always and practiced everywhere by all people. Are the "golden rule" and monogamy universal givens of rightness for everyone, Christian or not? The first way of thinking says, "Yes." Such are given, fixed, intended and forever realities.

The other way of thinking is more *inductive*. It assumes that "truths" are more subjective and situational realities that depend on personal and historical circumstance. Thinking works upward from where and who we are to what we then can assume is right, at least for us and for now.

Common in our post-modern and highly subjective world is the assumption that the right is what's most proper at the moment. Inductively, it is assumed that oppressed people in society should be helped to achieve their rightful political and cultural liberation, what's clearly right for them. There should be a dramatic reversing of the established patterns of social rules established the majority people for their own benefit. Since ethics is largely "situational," the Christian priority may shift to another concern tomorrow.

The inductive approach always champions freedom. It assumes that liberation and uninhibited individualism are human rights from which we all are to think and toward which society always should work. Is this assumption a universal human given? What about the Christian call of Jesus to come and submit to him, implying that a spiritual "slavery" can become the richest experience of human freedom? Social oppression is one thing and spiritual oppression another. The first may need addressed in some settings and the second in all settings.

Followers of the deductive way of thinking believe that people, like teachers and police officers and armies, represent legitimate social authority and exist for necessary control of all violation and change. They work to maintain the established right and pass it. By contrast, inductive thinkers believe that teachers and police officers and armies represent the power to preserve the current establishment which often doesn't function in the best interests of the "lesser" members of the society. Things must change. The maintainers of the current wrong must be challenged.

Deductive thinking favors *transmission* of the established order from generation to generation, while inductive favors *transformation away from the privileged establishment order.* The first argues that the current decay of culture is a result of the decline of traditional morality. The other thinks it's their calling as freedom visionaries to be anti-establishment and anti-tradition change agents. Beneath the surface of American politics and religion today is an intense ideological struggle between these two competing worldviews and ways of thinking. We Christians must think again, but which way and toward what end?

Karl Marx spoke of religion as a social sickness, the "opiate of the people." It functions, he believed, to put people to sleep so they won't challenge the prevailing order of things. The Emperor Constantine elevated young Christianity to official status in the Roman Empire around 315 A.D., presumably because he thought it could function as a stabilizing social factor for an empire beginning to crumble. Church historians sometimes think of this political endorsement as the fall of the faith.

How can Christianity infuse positively and yet not be used negatively by the prevailing powers of the world? Politicians often seek to use faith communities for non-religious social and personal ends. Contemporary "evangelical" Christianity is presumed to have considerable political clout in the United States. This has been courted by numerous politicians for their own elections and agendas. It's very difficult to live simultaneously as citizens of a given political order of humans and of the kingdom of God, children of God and agents of Jesus.

Which Thinking Approach?

Which of the two general approaches to human thinking represents Christianity at its best, not in the eyes of politicians but in those of its Lord? Is Christian theology itself deduced or induced, *delivered* by God or *developed* by church leaders? Is the truth and the church's agenda what is divinely revealed or whatever appears favorable to human liberation at the moment? Are divine revelation and social relevance natural opposites? The answers are a complicated "yes" and "no." We need to think again.

We need not disavow the gifts of intellect in giving thought to their Giver. In fact, it's the vocation of the Christian to out-think the opposition. Let's begin trying. One assumption permeates the Christian tradition and now very much deserves our attention as we decide how best to think.

Who or what really controls world events, especially ultimately? Jesus once came back to Nazareth. What did his hometown people see? Apparently a local young man showing off after abandoning a widowed mother and impoverished siblings to go on some preaching adventure, elevating himself shamefully. They ran him out of town. Can we see the truth even when it's standing right in front of us?

So much goes on behind the scenes of history's flow. The holy life of true believers is to be guided by an often unseen holy hand. Christian holiness is embracing God's invisible guidance as wisdom for our own lives of faith (Ps 85; Isa 30). Who's in charge of events? Sometimes it seems like nothing and no one. However, the "mystery of Christ" is said to have been revealed by apostles and prophets through the Spirit of God (Eph 3:4-5). Is that mystery truth's foundation, the key to ultimate reality? If so, how can we gain a dependable understanding of it active in our time?

This revealed mystery is fundamental Christian thinking, quite deductive, reason enriched by faith. The deepest of God's intentions are at work even if often out of the sight. The full reality of what is real involves both foreground and background. Realizing that there is an eternal background to world events is what gives meaning and hope to this strange and often chaotic life of ours. Christian faith assumes that there is "revelation," a higher knowledge granted from on high. How can we access it and think properly about what it implies for our living? Critical theological work must now proceed to answer such questions.

Says Paul, "We look not at what can be seen, but at what cannot be seen, for what can be seen is temporary, but what cannot be seen is eternal" (2 Cor 4:18). Christian believers at least glimpse by faith what for now is largely out of sight. It's God quietly at work. In Jesus, time and eternity are understood to be fused. Jesus saw the whole of what was happening in his day, foreground and background. He belonged perfectly to both worlds, visible and invisible. To realize this and live in this light is to be holy as God is holy. Can we think this dramatic way of enriched reason![15]

We are to not be discouraged when forced to think in less than ideal circumstances and with uncertain outcomes. The writer of the biblical book of Ecclesiastes was tempted to think that life in this world is little more than dust helplessly blowing away in the wind. If that's so, the best we can do is live for the moment and enjoy what little we can. We must come to terms with life as it really is, often fickle, fragile, frustrating, and yet yielding at least flickers of hope because God is and is offering the flickers.

Note the little-noticed fact that the book of Ecclesiastes is placed in the Bible between the psalms of David and the prophecies of Isaiah. Did the ancient editors do this deliberately? Frustration with the frailties of our lives must hear the music and realize that the herald of great news is ready to trumpet from the mountaintop.

When really down, maybe we are called to look both ways. Look *back* and hear the singing of the grateful Hebrews finally freed from bondage (Ps 19:1-4). Then look *forward* to hear Isaiah's grand announcement that the people of God are about to be set free to go home because the future suddenly will open to them (Isa 60:4-5). When caught in the middle of apparent negatives, forced to think only in paradoxical terms, we must be aware that we are surrounded by past goodness and being offered future hope![16]

In the great confusion and dangers of our contemporary world, it's time to think again about faith in God and divine revelation. We must decipher the implications of postmodernism for the Christian gospel. We must claim this new context for Christ by embodying the Christian faith in ways that the new generations can understand. We must remember that the gospel of Jesus Christ has gone forth in every previous age of human history and managed to speak to the longings of people. How can Christian believers today become agents of the Holy Spirit for life-changing encounters with the God in whom all things have their origin and meaning?

Chapter Four

Mystery Guides Mastery

Once the true nature of God is determined, answers to many questions are more easily found, or at least more comfortably lived without. We never will *comprehend* the ultimate mystery, but that which we cannot fully know at least is gracious and enables an adequate *apprehension*.

There is to be no downgrading of the importance of the spiritual life of Christians or any excessive elevation of the role of reason in Christian belief. If Christians are to be taken seriously as witnesses to the contemporary relevance of Jesus, a balance must be maintained. Our times call for courageously warm hearts attached to consciously clear heads.[17]

We humans live with a difficult paradox. When reaching for the ultimate truth, we soon realize that we are seeking to master the great mysteries of life. We hope to obtain in our limited ways the unobtainable. Unfortunately, reductionism seems to be everybody's problem. We tend to claim successful achievement and management of that which is not achievable or manageable.

Atheists claim to be able to eliminate the ultimate God question from consideration. There simply is no "God." On the other hand, agnostics downgrade all supposed revelations of the ultimate, settling for being open to the God possibility but not knowing anything about it for sure. "Conservative" Christians tend to reduce their understanding of God to the boxes of their own limited creeds, spiritual experiences, and denominational understandings. "Liberals" often reduce God to a poetic expression of their own social ideals. There's a universal tendency to reduce to claimed understanding that which is beyond our capacity to fully understand.

None of us should create "God" or "no-God" in our own image. With our best reasoning and limited language, we try our best to master the Mystery which or who yet remains beyond our reach. The classic book *Your God Is Too Small!* by J. B. Phillips remains our wake-up call. When we think we know it all, we can be sure we know considerably less than we think.

Christian believers have relatively firm footing when convinced that we are not alone in our search for the truth. We are to be patient, cautious, and humble, of course, and yet we still can entertain the real possibility that there is reason for believing, reality for which we reach. In Christian perspective, the good news is that God is real. How do we know this? Because God *wishes to be known* and has provided a way for us to gain at least a basic understanding of what otherwise is beyond us. Believers hear Jesus saying, "I am the way!" "I and the Father are one." God has come in Jesus for our understanding of the God we can't know properly otherwise.

Proper knowing at least begins with this. "God is a *verb* present to relate more than a *noun* called monarch."[18] Jesus instructs us to address God not as Your Majesty, although he rules all creation without equal, or as Your Highness, although he clearly is high and lifted up, or as Your Honor, although he is the final judge of the living and the dead. Instead, we are invited to refer to God as *Our Father* who has come in love to relate and redeem.

What of the arrogant Caesars, the swaggering Genghis Khans, and the fearsome Alexander the Greats? I avoid more contemporary names to duck needless controversy. These all, the named and unnamed, had or a few now are having their brief times on the world stage before becoming only dust in their graves. They may deserve our admiration but only passing attention. All of them fall well below the level of being worthy of worship.

We are told, "Blessed are the meek for they shall inherit the earth." Meekness as defined by Jesus is not weakness, but self-control under pressure. Look especially at Jesus himself who was exceedingly meek, born a king who left his palace to dwell among common folk like you and me. He was murdered on a cross and stuck in a carefully guarded grave. According to all known facts, and his faith community that now has persisted into its third millennia, these human efforts at grave-guarding were futile human efforts to do the impossible.

What were they? They were merely human attempts to *contain the uncontainable*. If this is so, Jesus really was God-with-us, the only place where worship belongs.[19] If this is so, the Mystery behind all mysteries has been Self-revealed. That Mystery now should guide all our human efforts at a modest mastery of understanding life's origins, goals, and destinies.

The place to begin is to stop and absorb the wonder of this revealed Mystery, not first for analysis but for our own humble transformation. "I don't first want to account for the peculiar beauty of a rainbow trout in a riffle or a thunderstorm's magnetic terror. I simply want to enjoy them. They, like God, all knock me out of analysis and smack me clear into pleasure and awe."[20]

The Trinity of One

Christian faith gives qualified credence to both of the typical ways of human thinking described above, each in its own place and when implemented under divine guidance. The key is a delicate balancing of reason and spirit , both enabled by the God who assists us in knowing the nature and workings of God. Two types of theological expression can be noted, with God potentially actively Self-revealed in both.

Before there were formal theological *doctrines* among Christians, there were dramatic spiritual *experiences* from which the doctrines arose. This is *inductive* thinking, moving from the experience to the doctrine that attempts to explain and express the experience. In addition, there's the reverse, *deductive* thinking where one begins with an assumption that leads to its experience.

A key assumption of the Christian is belief that none of our spiritual experiencing that is Christ-centered is by mere human initiation. The virginal conception of Jesus is believed only because of prior belief that God was before anything else was. God could and likely would reach, initiate life, and later Self-reveal by restoring this life in the conception of Jesus. A God of love naturally would reach to enable such an amazing thing. The presence of Jesus on the human scene was God's idea and doing, regardless of the humans involved.

As the Bible also makes clear, God has Self-revealed and has thus been experienced as *Trinity*. Such complexity of human thought lies at the heart of a singularly ultimate reality and gives critical guidance to all other theological thought. Any Christian doctrine, when properly guided by the Self-revealing divine Mystery, will root in the complexity of these simple truths that comprise Trinity. They first were experienced spiritually before being expressed theologically.

God as *Father* is the foundational truth of all things in all times. God created and the creation is reflective of the very nature of the Creator. We are to think God's thoughts after him as God enables, not trying to think them up on our own for our own convenience in fulfilling our own wishes. What eternally has been still is and always will be. This basic claim is in contrast to the relativistic style of postmodern thinking.

God as *Son* is the incarnate (enfleshed) expression of the Father in our midst, once come physically for our instruction on who the Father really is and what our thoughts, standards, and expectations about God and life ought to be. To know the truth involves being in close personal relationship with Jesus *who is the Truth* present with us. We love only because we first have been loved. This reflects a postmodern assumption that truth tends to emerge in relationships within community.

God as *Spirit* is our divine interpreter and teacher, enabling us to understand our immediate life contexts and conditions from God's viewpoint and in light of what the Son has done to enable needed change. Our possible close relationship with the Father is through the Son and now enabled by the Spirit. Human reason requires such relatedness and guidance (inductive thinking not done alone but based on the deductive assumption). This is compatible with today's postmodernism in that it is quite reasonable while also being highly relational.

God as Self-revealed is not an all-determining, controlling, and detached monarch of the distant skies. Rather, God is to be known as the relational and loving Parent who chooses to be genuinely related to this world in sacrificial ways that address our deepest human needs. Though sovereign and holy, God allows the divine being to be touched by the fallen world, often suffering because of such touching (the cross of Jesus). The old Deism of modernism is to be replaced by a biblical understanding that is much older and yet as new as today's Spirit experience, a postmodern instinct brought to life.

God's very essence is reaching and interactive love. God exists as Father, Son, and Spirit, a community of love and mutuality always reaching and relating, creating and re-creating. The biblical God is no lonely being, but a singular communion, the dynamic and loving Triune One who wants and enables meaningful interaction with us. God stands above (Father), stoops below (Son), and forever stays nearby (Spirit).[21]

The Trinitarian God is the one eternal God who is our pentecostal presence and gift-giver (Spirit). God was in the burning bush encountered by Moses, the source of the hot coals that touched the lips of Isaiah, and ultimately the little infant crying in a Bethlehem manger. The Christian concept of "Trinity" did not arise initially from the thinking of early disciples of Jesus, Jews who knew of only one God. It arose from their prior experience of becoming conscious of the very present lordship of the risen Christ and also the very present power of Christ's ever-present Spirit who is the one, eternal, amazing "*I AM.*"

Those early disciples found themselves having to speak of God in awesome and yet paradoxical and immediate terms.[22] They knew there was an active and present plurality of the great Singularity, the One experienced as three, the three who always is One! Like them, it's now time for Christians to think again theologically! We must think the thoughts that God provides, in line with the acted-out thoughts of Jesus, with the Spirit of Jesus showing us the right mission for our time and gifting us for the tasks at hand.

Of course, God's thoughts are never quite ours (Isa 55:8-9). Still, God the *Father,* known best in the *Son,* Jesus Christ, is divine thinking brought right in front of us by the Spirit. To do Christian theology is to probe this thinking, seek to express it in meaningful terms for our times, and echo it in our life's actions. We need to be still, allowing God the *Spirit* to take us to the depths and show us the way of Jesus the Son. Having experienced this showing, the Spirit also will assist in enabling us to move from experience to doctrine, from private probing to public expression.

Simply Laughable

Opponents of God's revelation always have been numerous. This must not be surprising or distracting. Their ideas may be shallow, often are self-serving, and possibly very wrong, convincing to the largely unthinking public. Disciples of Jesus must be serious students of the Bible and prepared on that base to out-think and out-live all such opposition. It's time to *be* again, always accompanied by the Spirit who enhances our thinking, enlightens our Bible reading, and enables our "in-Christ" living. Quality Christian theologians are accompanied by this trinity of thinking, reading, and living.

We are to remain humble always, admitting that it's hard to think adequately about God. Our daily lives are bringing pressure that constantly keeps us from thoughtful living or serious Bible reading and contemplation and then effective theological communication. Much routine church life "dumbs us down," depresses our Spirit relationship, and misdirects our theological thinking. The resulting lack of adequate ideas truly rooted in our faith does great harm to Christian life. It isolates us from the active reality of what we say we believe. This is intolerable. It's time to think again, to recenter church life in the revelational richness of in-depth Bible reading and Trinitarian God encountering.

Rudolf Bultmann was regarded as one of the great leaders of twentieth-century religious thought. He once said: "It is impossible to use electric light and the wireless and to avail ourselves of modern medical and surgical discoveries and at the same time believe in the New Testament world of spirits and miracles." We agree with this response. "To anyone who has worked through the relevant arguments, this statement is simply laughable. It only shows that great people are capable of great silliness."[23]

Unfortunately, this kind of shallow thinking has dominated much of modern intellectual and professional life, even in the field of biblical studies and Christian theology. Jesus people are being called to out-think the numerous opponents of Christian faith, even those inside church walls. I'm hardly an outstanding Christian thinker of our time like Bultmann once was, but I have been instructed by some of the best and see the need to exercise hard thinking and encourage you to do the same. We must not get away from this biblical instruction. "Always be prepared to make a defense to anyone who calls you to account for the hope that is in you" (1 Pet 3:15).

To trust meaningfully in God today requires a focused way of thinking and speaking about God that explains and guides the Christian vision of life. Such thinking and language are present in the Bible and have been carefully crafted in the works of select Christian writers in recent times. The Spirit is speaking and we must be listening and learning. The potential impact of our Christian witness depends on the quality of our thinking and the credibility of our living.

Clear and Warm

One outstanding Christian philosopher of recent decades was David Elton Trueblood of Harvard, Johns Hopkins, and Stanford Universities. He models the way to think clearly as Christians in these complex times. I was personally influenced deeply by Elton, as he had been previously by the famous scholar Rendel Harris. Elton once observed Dr. Harris combine in a classroom the *warm heart* and the *clear head*. Great thought is arid and empty if not enriched by depth of soul.

Likewise, deep soul minus clear thought can get lost in sloppy subjectivity and convince few if any others. Elton observed Rendel, with no apparent self-consciousness in front of students, drop to his knees and pray vocally with the simplicity of a little child. Young Elton was struck by this unabashed piety in the life of a great thinker. It's a powerful and necessary combination of clear thinking and honest searching.

I was privileged to study under Dr. Trueblood and observed a similar combination of tough thinking and simple faith. Elton admitted seeking to be the C. S. Lewis on the American side of the Atlantic Ocean.[24] He once informed students in my nervous hearing that he preferred that we not speak in his class until the fog in our heads had cleared! Of course, I was intimated in the presence of this great Christian philosopher, although I relaxed as I came to sense his simplicity, his deep caring for students and his sincere and loving soul. He had been well formed into the image of Jesus and earned the right to our most careful listening. How the whole church needs this today!

As a modest reflection of Trueblood, nothing in these pages should be taken as downgrading the importance of the spiritual life of Christians, or of excessively elevating the role of reason in Christian belief. Far from it. If we Christians want to be taken seriously as witnesses to the contemporary relevance of Jesus, our times are calling for warm hearts combined courageously with clear heads, both then followed by life actions that reflect the reality of that clarity and warmth.

It's time to think again in our current postmodern environment. One rational tendency offers hope for reestablishing a proper relationship with God and then with the creation. It's a renewed openness to spirituality and mystery in the face of a world being dominated by technology and materialism. The best thinking finally should lead to a divine "Mystery" known to be beyond the range of mere human thinking. It is to be experienced before being expressed. Fortunately, according to the Christian faith tradition, it's a Mystery *wanting to be known* to the degree that our frail human capacities will allow and the Divine is willing to enable. A high degree of willingness is seen in the coming of Jesus.

It's also time to communicate effectively such important things. Trueblood learned that there is "no probability of impression without *expression*." So he taught and wrote extensively. Writing forces attention to the importance of clear thinking and careful wording, hopefully infused with the depth of warm, Jesus-infused hearts. We rejoice in the influence of those fellow believers who have gone before. We also must accept the responsibility of the holy task now falling to us, including even thinking about the limits of thinking. Observed a wise Christian brother, "What you are is God's gift to you; what you become is your gift to God."[25]

Chapter Five

Outlasting The Deviations

Honest doubt can be a helpful servant of maturing faith. We need to be agnostics first and then there is a chance at arriving at a sensible system of belief. It's time to turn the tables on the atheists. Their announcement of a universal negative (there is no God) is an arrogant overreach of possible human knowledge. –David Elton Trueblood, *While It Is Day*

Atheism in part is an unpaid bill of the church which too often has presented God as remote and unsympathetic and existing at humanity's expense. Often atheists refuse to believe because they have not been told about the real God of the Christian gospel who loves us freely, wants a joyous relationship with us, and is anxious to empower us for the best we were created to be. –Clark H. Pinnock, *Most Moved Mover*

If Trueblood and Pinnock are right (above), our task as biblical Christians is to outlast the deviations of human thinking about Christian faith. Atheists have no future long-term. Some of them exist only because the church has misrepresented God and turned people away. The biblical God draws in rather than pushes away.

We must not be outthought by shallow skeptics who dismiss Christian faith because of faulty logic that sounds meaningful to the average person on the street. We must stop being believers who leave our hats and minds in the coatroom when entering the church. It's crucial that we think again about the great and still relevant foundations of the faith!

The Christian tradition is honorable and enduring and potentially life-changing. We must be humble and thoughtful disciples, partners with the ever-thinking people of Jesus who are willing to engage the culture now around us. Jesus was never reduced to speechless irrelevance by the many selfish opponents he encountered, religious or secular.

Shifting Truth Perspectives

We have seen that human perspective flows back and forth on the nature of human knowledge about the great issues of life. The "Enlightenment" championed a confident use of reason and logic to enable humans to be changed and to change their societies for the better. It seemed reasonable to assume that the future would be more humane, just, advanced, more enlightened when "liberated" humans took charge. Reason and logic were judged universally valid, with their laws applying equally to any thinker and all societies.

Influenced heavily by the terrible experience of World War I, with its extreme selfishness and brutality, post-modernists began seeking to replace this optimistic Enlightenment perspective. Far more pessimistic and relativistic, for them reason and logic came to be seen as merely conceptual constructs valid only for the established intellectual traditions in which they were created and used. There are, they judged, no views of reality that are objective, universally true or false.

It may not be possible for human beings to know things with certainty. There may be no moral values that are absolute and apply equally to all. Science and technology (and even reason and logic) are not necessarily vehicles of human progress but suspect instruments of established power. Humans can be so brutal to each other!

More than we would wish, the Christian community, especially in the "developed" Western world, has tended to follow this shifting of perspective. "Liberalism" tried to rid Christian faith of old dogmatisms and leaned more toward a "situationalism" of creeds and ethics. "Fundamentalism" reacted defensively and turned toward legalisms and rigid belief structures for Bible believers. End-time perspectives were influenced sharply. Future expectations of the Bible came to be understood far more pessimistically.

There was a general move after WWI from a *post*-millennialism (much reality of the Kingdom of God can be realized in this world *before* the return of Jesus) to a more pessimistic *pre*-millennialism (evil in this world is so strong that Kingdom realization will have to wait *until* the return of Jesus). Increasingly popular now is an *a*-millennialism (Kingdom realization being viewed much less in political terms regardless of time framework).

The "enlightened" modernity era lasted for less than a dozen generations, while orthodox Christianity already has flourished for more than four hundred generations and shows no sign of fatal fatigue. Even so, Christian orthodoxy ("straight" thinking about classic Christian believing) seems like a newcomer to today's cultural elites.

There is a little comfort in this observation. "Contemporary cultures present no tougher intellectual challenges to Christianity than did the fall of Rome, the collapse of the medieval synthesis, the breakup of the unity of Christendom in the sixteenth century, or the French Enlightenment. Christian teaching must be pursued today amid a similar collapse of modern assumptions."[26]

What has come after modernity is the yet-unclear postmodernity. What's next? No one really knows. Whatever it is, it will not succeed in destroying the deep roots of Christian memory and meaning. History argues that whatever the new human sidetracks, experiments, and deviations from classic Christianity, the seeds of God's good news in Jesus Christ already are planted and every culture, dying or being born, will see some of its growth.

Two outstanding Christian theologians have argued persuasively that Christianity remains a viable and thoughtful option for contemporary Christians. It must not lose its moorings as happened in its extreme liberalism, nor must it resort to the blind faith and hyper-rationalism of its old fundamentalisms. We must think carefully today about finding the proper middle way.[27]

This searching and adapting process goes on outside and inside the Christian faith community. Recall the recent and dramatic faith-life story of Christian theologian Thomas Oden. It has two major phases, one going as far from home as he could and then at last "inhabiting anew my own original home of classic Christian wisdom." He roamed widely, experimented often, and found himself reading the New Testament "entirely without its crucial premises of incarnation and resurrection."

Finally, Oden experienced a pleasant dream. He was wandering in a cemetery and suddenly encountered his own tombstone. It read: "He Made No New Contribution to Theology." He awakened "refreshed and relieved."[28] He was home again, back on classic ground and not trying to discover or invent dramatic new forms of faith alternatives. So, as Pinnock and Trueblood say above, it's time *to think again*, to turn the tables, make clear that atheism is an illogical sidetrack on the human quest for ultimate truth.

To be convincing, the grand scale of biblical revelation must be revisited, and on its own terms and not distracted or intimidated by "modern" sensibilities. Oden observes in *After Modernity...What?* that the Christian intellect has no reason to be intimidated in the presence of later-stage modernity. Christianity has seen too many "modern eras" to be cowed by this one.

Jesus always was prepared to respond to loaded questions thrown at him with disorienting questions of his own. Skeptics who make their harsh points have serious reasoning faults of their own. The people of Jesus are fragile and vulnerable witnesses to a "modern" world whose time is limited. Rather than huddle defensively, Christians ought to be prepared to respond gently but clearly and boldly. What we have to say has stood the tests of time and addresses relevantly the personal and social needs of our day and of any day.

Faithful followers of Jesus are to think deeply and then respond at each opportunity with the reasons for and results of believing. Those first disciples of the *crucified* Jesus hid behind closed doors, thinking they might be next. After they were met by the *resurrected* Jesus, no one could shut them up, and still must not!

Should We Be Up-To-Date?

Being "modern," up-to-date, always religiously contemporary is hardly the proper way to be. Life has very shallow meaning when designed to be in step with any fashionable time adored by the unthinking public. After all, every today is already morphing rapidly into some replacement tomorrow. Keeping in step now may be a laughable position tomorrow. The one "wedded to his time will soon be a widower!"[29] Those countering the legitimacy of Christian faith in our modern time are somewhat right while fundamentally wrong.

They confidently claim that today is the "post-Christian" era. Yes it is, and then also not at all.

Would you stand on a picket line waving your banner and yelling, *"Christendom has fallen, Long live Christ!"* Christendom is, after all, something quite different from Christianity. It's the administrative power structure, the institutionalization of the Christian religion constructed by believers. The founder of Christianity was Christ while the founder of Christendom is often said to be the Emperor Constantine some three centuries later. What's floundering currently is not Christ's Christianity but Constantine's Christendom, which we could say was abolished even before it began.

Jesus stated clearly that his kingdom is *not of this world*. Constantine, on the other hand, decided as a matter of political policy to favor and even strategize with the church for the worldly good of his empire—one that eventually collapsed. Our contemporary barbarians are dismantling Christendom, calling for the dethroning of its God and undermining all its certainties. That's being done in the name of the health, wealth, and happiness of humankind. The kingdom of Christ, however, is not vulnerable to this onslaught. No need to be up-to-date here.[30]

The world is littered with the debris of past human civilizations. This applies to utopias of every kind, whatever their ideologies. Why should anyone expect Christendom to go on forever? We must remember the year A.D. 410 when Saint Augustine learned that Rome had been sacked. He dared to envision this. "All earthly cities are vulnerable. Men build them and men destroy them. At the same time, there is the city of God which men did not build and cannot destroy." His masterpiece, *The City of God*, shows us how to cope with the collapse of any spent civilization, even Christendom. If spent, be confident that its heart beats on.

Today certainly is "post" in that Christianity has lost control of the general culture in the West. That's the surface truth, and it can be argued that the church is largely to blame and shouldn't be making power moves to be in control of public cultures in the first place. The larger truth is that in Jesus the kingdom of God still is drawing near, inviting a "pre" rather than a "post" mentality. Whatever is gone doesn't change the fact that God's "kingdom" always is on the verge of being brand new, a grand hope hovering just over the horizon of human experience.

Why might the church itself be partly to blame for its loss of cultural significance? The demise is not because there no longer are good reasons for the faith to be honored. It's more because shallow and sub-par thinking has gripped the popular mind, even the minds of many Christian believers. Selfishness is prevailing. It's an easy road to drift on, a "worldly" hole now mirrored by the "prosperity" gospel popular in many mega-church Christian congregations. It's time for believers to think again!

If the sloppy and selfish thinking of the skeptics is successfully countered, today may again be "pre-Christian," one on the verge of a major Christian revival. A world where anything goes eventually morphs into a world going nowhere except toward its own collapse. People stuck in that soon find themselves open to almost any alternative if it's presented believably and lived responsibly. Today may be a *pre-Christian* time like that of the early church if we are willing to think carefully and live well the faith we proclaim.

Elton Trueblood said repeatedly that the Christian faith is "an anvil that has worn out many hammers. A faith that could survive in spite of the condescension of the Greek thinkers, the fierce opposition of Roman emperors, the blight of the Dark Ages, and all the challenges of the modern world is not likely to just disappear in our time."[31] The Christian who thinks carefully about the faith in today's secular environment can be a forerunner of a better tomorrow, a genuine *radical* who challenges the widely accepted assumption that truth is only relative to one's self and one's wishes and times.

When the world was trying to put itself back together on some sounder footing after World War II, Trueblood was attempting to assist Christians in rethinking the faith and where it should fit into things "modern." He was seeking to imagine a pattern of life that's both timely and timeless. He knew that such a pattern would have to be more than a simple-minded effort to restore the past. It at least would have to out-think the false assumption that the past is now gone and meaningless for the new day.

We now need to rejoin John the Baptist down by the Jordan River. He will sound quite out of step while being right n step. Listen for that divine voice still saying, "You are my Son, with you I am well pleased" (Lk 3:22). Soon this Son, baptized by John, was proclaiming that in his coming the kingdom of God had drawn near, good news indeed! These prophetic words of grand announcement are still sounding for those willing to hear.

If the writings of Trueblood are rarely rivaled for their combination of both quality head and heart, one contemporary rival may be Dallas Willard. Says Richard Foster, "Rarely have I found an author with so penetrating an intellect combined with so generous a spirit. Clearly, he has descended with the mind into the heart, and from this place he touches us, both mind and heart."[32]

That's what we so much need today, a Jesus-shaped inner life explored and expressed with quality thinking that engages and impacts the culture of our time. We need Elton and Dallas again and again, whatever their names might be where you are.

Conjunctive Aliens

The "conjunctive" nature of John Wesley's theology runs deep and is a good model. God's truth is said to be so grand that it transcends our rational tools and categories. Still, the twin reality is that ultimate truth is fundamentally reasonable even while being profoundly personal. Theological dialogue must include many voices, past and present, global and local, West and East, and move across cultures to bring Scripture into engagement with its many contextual challenges. Disciples of Jesus must experience, think, and live well. These three must join, interpenetrate. They are to be one whole, not separated or any neglected.

For example, the effective struggle for social justice requires biblically faithful communities of justice-seeking Christian disciples who can both think strategically and bear well in their persons and actions the real image of Jesus. The church always has been most faithful when it's gone back to its biblical roots. When it does, it's freed to be most creative in challenging the spiritual, social, and economic crises of the day.

Going back to basics is being "radical" in the proper way.[33] It's insisting that intended fruits come only from honoring proper roots. Wesley did just this with his moving over time toward a normative use of the New Testament and regular reference to the life and practices of the early church, informed by both the Western (more rational) and Eastern (more experiential) traditions of the faith.

The church is to be a colony of heaven on earth, an island of one culture in the middle of another. This colony will be different indeed and yet relate well and make a difference. The meaning of Christian baptism is supposed to be a public transferring of personal citizenship from one dominion to another, making the new believer a willing *resident alien*.[34] Paul told the Philippian church, and now us, to "have this mind among yourselves which is yours in Christ Jesus." Our "commonwealth is in heaven" (3:20).

In this dramatic context of new citizenship, in this Spirit world of new creation, believers in Jesus gain increased ability to think more effectively about the things of life and death, meaning and destiny. There is increased competency, not from human ability but Spirit provision. We must glimpse and then evidence a new reality.

Here's a beautiful image. "The church rides the wind of God's Spirit like a hawk endlessly and effortlessly circling and gliding in the summer sky. It ever pauses to wait for impulses of power to carry it forward to the nations. The main rationale of the church is to actualize all the implications of baptism in the Spirit."[35]

We believers in the risen Jesus must come to see clearly the twin mistakes of placing exclusive trust in the experience of the present or the past. The person concerned only with what is gone is hardly alive. The one concerned only with the present has a life essentially empty of content. If we reject ideas from an earlier century only because they are earlier, logically we are driven to reject those of the past year or even the past hour. Clear thinking must follow its own course wherever that leads, including to enduring elements of yesterday.

Persons committed only to the contemporary are like the shallow Athenians who, at the time of Paul's visit to Athens, were spending their time always telling or hearing *something new* (Acts 17:21).[36] This is a quickly passing pursuit, a curious exercise in little but novelty.

We now are faced with an awareness of two things that unfortunately are in conflict. Serious thinking is crucial to in-depth and defensible believing, something so needed today. In spite of this, humans have a tendency to live by uninformed and self-serving perceptions that fly in the face of clear logic.

I have watched several televised U. S. presidential "debates" on television. They are hardly serious debates, rather more exercises in spinning scripted perceptions of voter wants while evading direct answers to pointed questions. We must do what we can in such a shallow and office-seeking world, leaving the result in the hands of God. Let's at least dare to think carefully again! God would love an honest debate on any subject.

Turning the Tables

C. S. Lewis impacted the thinking of David Elton Trueblood primarily because he "turned the intellectual tables." The Quaker philosopher had been accustomed to a world in which the sophisticates engaged in attack while Christians sought bravely to be defensive. Lewis turned this around and forced the unbeliever into a posture of defense. In the *Screwtape Letters* he inaugurated a new Christian strategy, forcing the unbeliever into a corner. However vulnerable the Christian position may be, it was announced that the position of the opposition is more vulnerable still. Good thinking!

The opponents of Christianity suppose that they have a monopoly on reason, while the Christian has nothing to rely on except raw faith. Lewis reversed this assumption. Screwtape, the arch Devil, advised his nephew about the handling of a person who is weakening in his atheism and somewhat attracted to Christ. "Tell him that above all he *dare not let the fellow think.*" If he thinks, says Screwtape, he will be lost to us! This intellectual straightforwardness of Lewis made Trueblood see more clearly and act more boldly.[37]

One day I was sitting as a new student of Elton Trueblood's at Earlham School of Religion. He caught my attention by announcing, very much in C. S. Lewis style, that atheism is not a respectable intellectual position. Why? Because it tries to affirm absolutely a universal negative, there is no God, when definitive evidence is wholly lacking for such a claim and human rationality is incapable of such an infinite reach. Even so, the twisted Screwtape lives on.

Given the presence of Jesus Christ on the human scene, the exact opposite of atheism must be given due consideration. Reverent agnosticism keeps us from talking easily about what *cannot be*.[38] Maimonides once said, "Do not imagine that these great mysteries are completely and thoroughly known to any of us."

Even so, there are many features of the known world that can be readily understood with a theistic hypothesis, and hardly with any other. These features form a chain of verification of belief in God. Granted, individually none of these arguments for God's existence are absolutely convincing, although together their cumulative effect is considerable. Some faith always is required (also true of any alternative faith stance).[39] Let's think again and dare to believe, openly, proudly, not defensively.

The challenge for today's Christian believers is to realize that, if God truly is, all truth necessarily flows from the divine nature and somehow is built into the very fabric of the creation. Our very human ability to reason is a gift from some "above," an ability that is a responsibility as well as a danger-filled process. The reasoning of the skeptics is clearly vulnerable. Therefore, let's relax and move on in confident faith.

Thomas Oden insisted that the best reasoning of Jesus believers must be in community with the classic Christian tradition of the early centuries. Reason alone has its limits and easily becomes used for selfish purposes and twisted by contemporary circumstance. If we are to be mature spiritual beings and effective Christ witnesses, we must be thoughtful and humble as we seek to bring the classic consensus of the faith to bear on the modern scene. We certainly aren't the first quality thinkers in the community of Christ.

Chapter Six

Being Caught Between

The Scriptures are a reliable and sufficient guide to Christian life. The truth of the Bible lies in what it intends to say about the history of human salvation, not in our curiosity about God's view of modern science, psychology, or sociological theory. The sufficiency and reliability of the Bible lies "in all things pertaining to salvation." There's no need to defend the Bible in areas that it never meant to address authoritatively.

There often is a selectivity in the portions of biblical truth that manages to get recognized and proclaimed. A tunnel-visioned halfway theology is flooding the airways and invading prominent pulpits. It's an open door to religious fanaticism, basic theological misunderstandings, and eventually a general weakening of the impact of Christians on civilization.[40]

Brother Crispin, a Franciscan monk in New York City, once told a non-Catholic guest about his having to expel one of the men from a homeless shelter. The friars have a strict zero-tolerance policy and the man was back on drugs, so reluctantly he was banished to the streets. "I thought you guys were nice," said the surprised guest. "We're not nice. We're *kind*. Jesus told us to be wise as serpents and innocent as doves."[41]

Wisdom and love are a complex combination. Love always is to include wisdom, or as Tolstoy said, "Love cannot be stupid." Love always is kind, which apparently doesn't necessarily mean being naively nice. Paradox is complex by definition. Real life often forces us to realize that we humans are caught between. The in-between is not always the positioning of opposites awkwardly stuck together.

Both wings may be essential for a bird's effective flight. Both elements of a Christian paradox are true, while each is more true when in careful combination with the other.

The Wisdom of Block Logic

Block logic is a common literary device often found in the Bible. Concepts not appearing to fit together rationally are blocked together as though they do. When they are, a fuller truth appears. God hardened Pharaoh's heart, the same heart Pharoah himself had hardened. Jesus is both the Lamb of God and the Lion of the tribe of Judah. There is divine "predestination" alongside human free will. Which is the truth in these and other cases of combination? The best answer is "yes."

The whole truth is found in the paradox of parallel truths. This way of thinking is not easily accepted by today's Western world that's too scientifically minded to allow what appears on the surface to be illogical.[42] Real life, however, cannot be described in any simple formula. Biblical teaching isn't always "simple," just realistic because of its wholeness.

The Hebrews behind much of the biblical development were humble enough to recognize that the fullness of truth is not readily available in the neat rational packages we mere humans like. One plus one does not equal three, but 8-6 might get the right answer even though quite a different process on the face of it.

It's teasingly said that three rabbis arguing can fill a room with five different opinions. How? Two of them don't agree with themselves! Such things appear paradoxical, even contradictory, but are best blocked and jointly embraced, not pulled apart. When they are, two truths can become one lie.

The God who will welcome us at the end of the faith journey is the same God who will walk with us every step of the way to that end. Jesus was the great Teacher and also the primary subject of his own teaching. God is fully revealed in Jesus and yet always beyond our full comprehension even when knowing Jesus. Christian faith is centered in divinely-revealed truth and historic witness, and also is one that is ever new in our experience and understanding.

This block logic mentality is what G. K. Chesterton once called "the romance of orthodoxy." To be "orthodox" in Christian belief means to thinking *straight* and *whole*. Thinking straight is easier and much more common than also thinking whole. Whole means approaching Christian truth with broad perspective, having appreciation for the intricate interrelatedness of strands of meaning, being patient and recognizing more than the latest discovery, loudest voice, or most popular creedal formula.

Partial truths and unbalanced theologies are everywhere. It's time for a renewed biblical commitment to the wholeness of thought and action. We need rooted and relevant theological equilibrium. Being caught between truths may not be the most comfortable position, but it tends to be the most biblical stance and thus the best way to proceed.

Truth lies more in the broader whole and less in its separated parts and pieces. What God seeks to join together let us not wrench apart. All of the core truths of Christianity are paradoxes. We must find the patience to avoid abortive choices and begin to celebrate being *caught between truths*. When the fullness of truth is found in paradox, a pairing of parallel truths, the challenge is obvious. To begin, the Bible itself is a paradox to be handled with great care. It's both an obvious human production and a marvelous divine revelation. Which? Both!

It's common to possess strands of the truth and fail to see the whole of the tapestry. Precious truth strands are all the more beautiful and true when linked with care to the alternate strands on the edges of our inadequate thoughts and experiences. This is thinking that postmodern people can understand and appreciate. It's communal, relational, cautious, appreciative-of-diversity thinking.

The Piecemeal Approach

Is God forgiving love or final judge? Yes. Was Jesus truly human or actually God with us. Yes. Is the Bible a human production or divine revelation? Yes. Is the church the Body of Christ or an assembly of fragile and immature believers? Yes. And so it goes. We are caught between believing and doubting, visioning and failing to fully achieve our own vision.

Our believing requires the best use of human reason, even while there remains mystery that exceeds our reasoning ability. On this side of heaven, reaching for the whole truth will be somewhat like looking into a heavily frosted mirror (1 Cor 13:12). We will see and yet not see. Let's never insist that what little we can see is definitely the whole truth!

Many believers settle for a piecemeal approach to the content of their faith. In this way, one easily can lie by focusing only on a small portion of a larger truth. The guilt is lack of proper association, the perverted ability to lie with parts of the truth. Heresy is rarely unadulterated falsehood. It's usually something not altogether untrue, just false because the fullness of the truth is missing. Half of the truth can be little better than no truth at all. For instance, Jesus was a real baby, very human. Yes, but *is that all*? To report only one truth is to miss the amazing larger truth of Jesus also being God with us in flesh. Dare to think broadly and believe fully.

A common criticism of denominationalism is that it's an institutionalized epidemic of majoring in minors, groups of believers organized around the same Bible being used to prove each other wrong. We learn in Acts 18:25 that Apollos was an eloquent man with high motives and persuasive techniques, although he knew "only the baptism of John." What devastation can be brought by a skillfully presented half portion of the truth. It's so possible to lie even though all that is said is the truth, just announced with the impression that it's the whole truth when it isn't.

This can get very personal. A close friend of mine was shot to death in a hunting accident. At the funeral, three different ministers tried as tenderly and logically as they could to explain to the weeping relatives that God controls and ordains all things but does not cause and is not responsible for many tragic events happening within that divine providence. How difficult it is when the precise truth often is discovered only in a delicate imprecision.

The fullness of truth involves wonder and mystery, complicating the attempt at a final intellectual definition. It's like that peace which "passeth understanding." We rest in the assurance even after our reason has given up on full explanation. Our world is reasonable, but not quite. It's understandable, at least to a degree.

We do know for sure that any "god" we claim to understand fully is a mere idol fashioned in our own image. What we have in Christian faith is less a cosmic Fact delivering to us a catalog of scientific facts about itself and more a Person, indeed a Heavenly Father who has come to us intimately, personally, in a way beyond simple definition. What is God? God is not a *what* but the ultimate *Who*, the unspeakable "*I AM.*"

God has encountered us along the paths of our historical existence, calling for our faithful response as human persons to the divine Person. This is so enveloping of all meanings simultaneously that it's most appropriate to mere logic and narrative. We must burst into song, rely on poetry, resort to the use of parables and paradoxes. Jesus often did. So must we.

The classic creeds of Christian church history are milestones in the crucial art of theological equilibrium. Modern Christians like Kevin W. Mannoia have been both serious thinkers and humble believers, anchored in Christian roots while reaching in Christian mission.[43]

We are not to choose between such dual commitments since both are required. One is implied in the other. "In formal logic, a contradiction is a signal of defeat, but in the evolution of real knowledge, it marks the first step in progress towards a victory."[44] Here is clarity about the importance of accepting a lack of clarity!

Christians today must be willing to orchestrate the paradoxes presented by the mixture of human experience and divine revelation. Only a "full" gospel is really the truth. By being caught between truths, the believer can enter more fully into the whole of truth itself. Only here, in the in-between, do we have real understanding of what it means to be "orthodox" believers. That center place is where the Spirit of God works and true Christian unity lies. It's a place actually believable to today's post-moderns.

Orthodoxy is the theological stance that feels the pull of the competing elements of a given subject, keeps them from flying apart, and thus keeps them most fully true. We are being called to search for the *whole counsel* of God and not fall prey to the persistent temptation to affirm the convenient, familiar, partial, and comfortable, ignoring "classic" elements that deserve recognition and are costly if ignored.

The Protestant Principle and the Bible

The so-called "Protestant Principle" is worth understanding and following. It forbids giving anything human a place of ultimacy in the church. No creed, organizational structure, person or group of persons, custom, habit, or idea, nothing human is to be allowed supremacy. Positively put, the Protestant Principle puts forward as the only absolute the sovereignty of God expressed in the good news of Jesus Christ.

Proper commitment is to the sovereignty of divine grace, not to any particular expression of it or theological reflection on it. Since many things are constantly trying to assume control in church life, Protestantism at its best insists that reformation must be an ongoing characteristic of church life. The postmodern mind can appreciate and actively encourages this insistence. It evidences being alive, humble, broadly perceptive.

The church should be an open fellowship of continuous conversation about what the Spirit is saying to the Son's people about the Father's will and ways. The goal of Bible reading is less to find answers to all of our spiritual and ethical and strategic questions. It's to be more of a tool for reshaping its readers into the image of God's Son. We are to go to the biblical text realizing that it intends to come to us so that we might come back to God. More than merely reading the Bible to be informed, we are to read it to be changed.

This Protestant Principle includes not making an idol of the Bible itself. Scripture is no ultimate revelation merely as a sacred written document. Although it is the primary vehicle of Christian truth today, it's not the full truth *in and of itself*. It's the reliable source of instruction, the appointed agent for properly approaching the one true God now Self-revealed in the Son, Jesus. The reliability of Scripture is not resident in its mere words.

This Principle insists that Scripture becomes binding for faith and practice through the internal witness of the Holy Spirit, whose voice is heard best in the community of faith, the church. Scripture speaks understandably and savingly only as the Spirit enlivens it and witnesses to the meaning of its truth for current lives and circumstances. Apart from this witness of the Spirit, the Bible is little more than another religious book of ancient origin.

Scripture clearly remains the central source of the memories, symbol systems, hopes, teachings, metaphors, and paradigms by which the Christian community originally came into being and has continually refreshed and renewed itself over the centuries. The interpretive witness of the Spirit of God, however, did not cease with the canonization of Scripture long ago but continues providing a guiding light for our understanding, experiencing, and applying of its sacred pages.

Here's the necessary caution to discipline extremes. No fundamentally new or different knowledge will emerge in the Spirit's contemporary speaking beyond that which already is revealed in Scripture.[45] Since the Teacher is the Spirit *of Christ*, all lessons that arise now will be consistent with who Christ is and what he intended to teach when with us in the flesh. The inspiring Spirit is that *of Jesus*, who was, is, and always will be the same faithful presence of the Father.

Perhaps the best word to describe the authority of the Bible is "sufficiency," a word found in Scripture about itself. Paul reports that God said to him, "My grace is *sufficient* for you, for power is made perfect in weakness" (2 Cor 12:9). Christians should be content with the Bible that God has given and not alter it to the way we prefer.

Granted, it would be convenient and satisfying to have a "perfect" text, a literary product errorless in all ways, but this is wishful thinking projected on the real Bible by modernistic arguments not found in the sacred text itself. Such thinking defies the Protestant Principle and distracts from the Bible's actual purpose, our salvation.

Some insist loudly, "If the Bible isn't perfect, nothing in it can be trusted!" I respond this way. The Spirit was originally in the Bible, inspiring its production, and now is in it illuminating its proper understanding. The Spirit is of God, and God can be trusted. The Holy Spirit who originally moved people to speak in ways that led to the biblical writing (2 Pet 1:20-21) is the same Spirit who now guarantees the *sufficiency* of the Bible for God's original and current salvation intent, our most pressing spiritual need. There is no error in any of that.

The Gender of God

We Bible readers today must remain open to new learning and insights, results that may not fit with current "facts" as judged by the public. There always should be "protest" against any wooden fixedness of reading and interpreting the Bible. The Spirit's presence keeps it a living and always relevant Word. Human scenes and divine strategies keep changing. God's being and intent, however, is forever fixed and unchanging.

Human language and the shifting cultural backgrounds of the original writers and present readers of the Bible clearly present a continuing challenge for proper biblical interpretation. Language shapes significantly how we humans think. We always are needing to think again! For instance, what about thinking of God in particular gender language? The Bible evolved in a patriarchal world, so masculine language tends to dominate.

The Bible clearly reveals God as living, speaking, and personal, but never as "he" or "she" in essential being. The second commandment forbids humans making God in the image of any earthly thing, women or men included. The actual reality of God is beyond everything we humans can conceive (Isa 55:8–9; 1 Cor 2:9–13). Language is a troubling tool, inadequate to capture fully the God who precedes it and yet seeks to be known in part through it.

God reflects the best characteristics of each human gender without ever being either. We speak about God as the Father of the Son who comes to us in the man Jesus, and as the Spirit who is the Spirit of the Father and Son. Never is anything here talking about the gender *of* God. We are using language analogies from human experience to talk about the kind of relationships that exist between members of the divine Trinity and between the Triune God and us human beings.

How careful we must be not to use our language analogies to be unjust to each other by insisting that one human gender, male or female, is superior to another.[46] God loves all equally, calls all graciously, and gifts all as these callings require.

It's surely best to allow Jesus to show us how to interpret the Bible. He taught us how to see, what to emphasize, and also what could be deemphasized or even ignored. Obviously, he was in no way a fundamentalist or literalist. He was a man of the Spirit and openly handled the Hebrew Scriptures in a particular way. He "consistently ignored or even denied exclusionary, punitive, and triumphalistic texts in his own Jewish Bible in favor of passages that emphasized inclusion, mercy, and honesty."[47] We then should be careful and follow his lead.

Membership: Mainline or Reform?

Even in our church affiliations, we believers find ourselves caught between. Often the choice is opting for a mainline denomination of Christians or a critical reform movement currently challenging the religious establishment. The best choice likely will be paradoxical, "yes, both." If one is a loyal denominational believer, that member should know the strengths of the affiliated denomination, why it came into being originally, and what real contributions it may have for the fuller health of today's larger Christian community. Such knowing and health working is at the heart of membership legitimacy.

Affiliation should keep a loving eye on the whole people of God and champion the gifting potential of the affiliated body for the health of the whole. A helpful distinction is between the "T" and the "t's" of the Christian community across the centuries. The first is *the* Tradition, basic, overarching, the whole body of Christ. The latter are the *t's*, the segments of the whole hoping to live within and contribute something of significance to the whole.

By contrast, reform church movements are bodies of believers reacting negatively to the common downsides of denominations. They are freshly envisioning the whole and hoping to restore to the "T" its wholeness and not represent in any ingrown fashion only a partial and flawed reflection of the whole by a divisive separateness. Both the mainlines and reformists must remain aware that their existence can deteriorate easily into a cult-like separateness that God detests.

We believers are not to drive a wedge between the "structural" and the "prophetic," or in biblical terms the priestly and prophetic.

Both always are present and we must be carefully caught between. The mistake is assuming that the work of the Holy Spirit is located exclusively in one or the other, with our trying to take control of managing the church by championing one and decrying the other.

This tendency to "apostacy" must be thought about again. It's God's church, not ours. Christian unity is a big deal for post-modern believers. Maintaining the dynamic of the church's legitimate life is the work of the Spirit. The Spirit ministers through established priests and structures and also cleanses through prophetic voices. The Spirit of God constitutes, gifts, and guides the church.

When we view the mission of the church from the standpoint of "a generous pneumatology," we can "relinquish control and open ourselves to all that God is doing through prophetic leaders and movements *and* through the church's established structures. We are free to hold with open hands all that God has given to the church for carrying out God's mission to the world. We are free to celebrate and enjoy the one gift that really matters, namely the transforming presence of the Holy Trinity in the midst of it all."[48]

Chapter Seven

Wisdom Uses A "Quad"

"I want their hearts to be encouraged and united in love, so that they may have all the riches of assured understanding and have the knowledge of God's mystery, that is, Christ, in whom are hidden all the treasures of wisdom and knowledge. I am saying this so that no one may deceive you with plausible arguments" (Col 2:2-3, NRSV).

If truth is to be known whole in the church, in its complexity that includes knowledge of "God's mystery," and in ways alive and relevant for our times, the manner of the Christian's coming to know will itself have to be complex. That's often called the "Quad."[49]

If true in the one-hundred-yard dash, it's also true in quality Christian thinking and believing. The original posture, the positioning and angle of the initial lunge forward have much to do with who will be on the winner's stand. Begin thinking with the wrong presuppositions and the battle already is lost.

If one accepts the assumption that there is no objective truth behind morality, no grounding for ethics, no fixed standard for judging right and wrong, the thinker is boxed into a position where there can't be a reasonable discussion about "sin." The very idea of wrongdoing has been rendered meaningless. Actions then are branches with no roots or intended fruits. They are just disconnected thoughts and actions.

A Christian believer must move beyond holding right religious concepts to being rooted properly in the larger truth that gives meaning to the "right." If there are ultimate roots, then there is a difference between right and wrong, proper and improper action, the intended fruit emerging from the particular root. Given the presence of deep Christian roots, there must be a knowing of the faith with the mind and an expressing of it in all of life, yielding Christ-like fruit.

Christian faith should be right belief (*orthodoxy*), right heart (*orthokardia*), and right practice (*orthopraxis*). One can hold correct opinions and still be a stranger to the religion of the heart. One certainly can do right things for the wrong reasons. As in baseball, there must be three bases achieved before one is ready for home plate. For the Christian, the three are more gifts of grace than skilled play on our own.

The church should be constituted by true believers committed deeply to all three of the "orthos." This requires being sensitive to the system of checks and balances comprising the "quadrilateral."[50] We will know only if we learn how to approach knowledge in dependable ways. That's faithfulness to the "Quad."

A "Personal" Approach

Two things came to dominate Professor David Elton Trueblood's teaching from early in his career. One was the professional goal of being a clear thinker. The other was honoring the needed logic sustaining his thought. He believed deeply that philosophy, like science, is not to be determined by psychological variables, but by evidence and logical consistency. Philosophy is the discipline of thinking carefully about thinking itself.

Trueblood's own philosophy was guided by this central belief. "If Christianity is not true, then it's an evil." It's not enough for a conviction to be comforting, satisfying some psychological need. It needs to be *true*.[51] He became convinced that atheism is an easy but thoughtless and unacceptable place of beginning really knowing. There are better options.

Where you begin your thinking, your choice of starting assumptions, has so much to do with where you will arrive. Aiming a rocket toward the Moon, if off course only a tiny bit in initial trajectory, could miss the target entirely. A wrong beginning magnifies the negative over time and distance. If there is no absolute standard of measurement and careful adherence to it, the cause is likely lost.

Openness to truth as being objectively real, and commitment to follow the quest wherever it leads, were assumptions behind the discipline practiced by Trueblood in his teaching years at Guilford College. The campus hosted weekly group meetings of about forty students each. They affectionately were called the "Heretics Club" because there was no limit to what could be discussed without embarrassment. Truth was in charge, whatever it is and wherever it goes.

Recalling the three "orthos," focus on the demanding requirements of being true and logical must not be merely an exercise in arid scholasticism. The Heretics Club started with what was considered the most important fact we know about our universe. It's the home of *persons*, suggesting that origins and destinies somehow are profoundly *personal*. There appears good reason to take Jesus seriously when he announced that he was the divine Person come to us from the Father. His person *is the truth* (Jn 14:6), very personal truth!

If Jesus was right, then somehow all truth flows from the realm of the personal, particularly from the personhood of the man from Nazareth. Our relationship with him will be key to an increasing awareness of who he is and what truth he brings in his very person. All this will come through more than refined thinking. It will come through the Spirit of Jesus who enables the re-formation of our very beings. We are to be new-creation persons, basic to really knowing.

This personal dimension of reality is the proper initial trajectory of knowledge apprehension. It's essential to the proper launching of our human philosophic and theological thinking. For Trueblood, it became the most compelling reason for believing that God, the Infinite Person, actually exists. Like C. S. Lewis, atheism then lost its credibility for worthy thinkers.

Logically, self-consciousness surely cannot be the product of meaningless unconsciousness. Who we are as thinking humans hardly can have come by pure accident from the inertness of dead nothingness. That's too big a stretch of faith for the carefully thinking person.

The work of Archbishop William Temple of England is a substantial place to begin. His thinking stands well in the face of the many strands of wayward modern thinking. One of the better Christian intellectual resources in modern times is Temple's *Nature, Man, and God*. It probes the totality of the Christian gospel in its various paradoxes. Personhood is in the lead, with the three orthos quite evident throughout.

Temple realizes that the fullness of the gospel of Jesus Christ must be both social and individual. He welcomes the insights of natural scientists, seeing them part of God's revelational pattern. He rejects all small conceptions of God and sees that nothing less than the concept of the *Infinite Person* is large enough to meet the requirements of critical thought.

Given Temple's influence, it's no surprise that the first academic work of Trueblood was the *Logic of Belief,* or that a pivotal later volume would be *A Place to Stand*. Jesus is seen as the Self who brought personal consciousness into being in the first place. Salvation for us humans comes through consciousness and acceptance of his person and work.

Jesus is the only sure place to stand as we seek to perceive the largest stretches of all reality. When we are in proper position, with feet planted on something truly solid, it's possible to launch out with confidence on the quest for knowledge.

The solid place of faith's beginning, according to the New Testament, is this. "Be united in love so that you may have all the riches of assured understanding and have the knowledge of God's mystery, that is, Christ in whom are hidden all the treasures of wisdom and knowledge. I am saying this so that no one may deceive you with plausible arguments" (Col 2:2-3).

The curriculum of my undergraduate alma mater, Geneva College, is based on a similar assumption. Christian education seeks to develop "the students' abilities to know God and relate themselves and the created universe to God through the study of His Word and works." Christian higher education emphasizes the person and work of the Lord Jesus Christ. Why? In order for students to see *in Christ* the ultimate purpose and meaning of the whole universe.

If all the treasures of wisdom and knowledge are hidden in the person of Jesus, why then the need for a "Quad"?

A Great Place to Begin

George Fox had the grand idea that Christian experience could be couched in *the present tense*. He discovered the power that emerges when someone moves from speculation to experience. Actual experience may be the only evidence convincing to postmoderns, the evidence of changed lives, real communities, and the appreciation of diversity in ways of knowing.

The "Quaker" tradition emerging from Fox was soon furthered by the intellectual work of Robert Barclay. He set forth a central paradox for intellectuals, one necessary but not always welcomed. It's that God has set aside the wise and learned, often the disputers and skeptics of this world, and instead chosen a few "despicable and unlearned disciples" (lesser only in letter-learning), as Jesus did fisherman of old. Barclay was in "the strong position of a scholar who could, when necessary, minimize the importance of scholarship."[52]

Followed later was the wise thought of John Wesley. A good overview is caught up in four words, beginning with the letters of *CARE*. Wesley was *C*atholic because not sectarian, *A*postolic because he sought to go back to the roots of the faith, *R*eformed because he wanted always to improve himself and the church whenever possible, and *E*vangelical because he was Christ-centered.

A favorite phrase of Wesley's was "holy conjunction." There should be a conjunction between clear thinking, tender hearts, and sacrificial service. Christian fellowships that rightly understand their identity in Jesus should know Scripture thoroughly *and* follow the Spirit wherever led in personal and social change. Believers are to be evangelistic about the gospel *and* socially active on behalf of the kingdom of Christ. One of the more important words that Jesus ever used was *and*. We are to worship in spirit *and* truth. Similar paradoxes should prevail.

Jesus was the man from Nazareth *and* the Son sent from the Father. The Bible is central to our human reception of divine revelation. On the other hand, it also is a human vehicle for conveying what is well beyond human comprehension.

Insistence on terminology like "inerrancy" of the original autographs (which we don't have) is an understandable reaction to modernist reductions of the Bible. Nonetheless, it also is an overreaction that can verge on idolatry when trying to absolutize rigid positions to the exclusion of necessary nuances. Quite unintentionally, one can manage to lie while telling too rigidly one of the more precious of the Christian paradoxical truths.

When Clark Pinnock and I were working together on *The Scripture Principle*, I cautioned about his wanting to continue using "inerrant" language when our work was qualifying it in multiple ways. He admitted that such was awkward but thought it still justified "politically." Many conservative "evangelicals" were strongly committed to the word even if well beyond our view of its technical legitimacy.

We decided that it was time to think again about the Bible's inspiration, even if still needing to honor language almost sacred to some. It was like preferring the King James Version of the Bible for the classic beauty of its language even if the best manuscripts and common tongue have gone well beyond the quality of the translation and effectiveness of its communication.

Let's begin in the proper place so we don't end up in the wrong place. The reflective Christian does well to admit upfront the possibility of being wrong. Christian convictions, strong as they may be in the face of the alternatives, always rest on faith and not absolute certainty. We are fallen sinners being saved by grace. What we often think we know could be coming from our own preference or ignorance or even fallen nature. Consider this caution:

> Faith without reason is an ally of theological dogmatism and religious superstition, bosom friends of error. But reason without faith is rationalism, which assumes that all reality must be verified, an assumption which is itself unreasonable. The universe is so vast and full of mystery that human reason alone is a puny instrument with which to relate ourselves to it. The wider our scope of knowledge becomes the more the mystery deepens.[53]

Caution coming from truth's complexity and our needed humility brings us to the important "Quad" concept. A "quadrilateral" is used by many Christians as a wise and careful approach to understanding the truths of the faith. It's a three-pronged approach to quality biblical reading and understanding. The four elements of the Quad are the Bible and the three available means of its accurate understanding for today.

The need for this quadrilateral comes from a simple fact. We humans learn things in various ways and need checks and balances to be sure that what we come to "know" is not just a conclusion coming from our own preference or ignorance or emotions or particular church background. The Quad sifts what we think we know in a careful attempt to avoid these common sources of inaccuracy.

Although the Quad suggests something with four sides, in this case it's really three. It's biblical authority being checked carefully by a trio of separate means that seek to assure quality reading and interpreting. Lacking use of any one of these checks can lead to serious error in biblical understanding. With the Bible as the primary agent of conveying the historic witness to God's Self-revelation in Jesus Christ, the three "checking" means provide necessary quality control.

We humans read and interpret the Bible in given settings (our *traditions*), with our available information and best logic (*reason*), and in light of our own life events, spiritual and otherwise (*experience*). Each of these three alone is quite inadequate. Together, they tend to ensure the best available biblical wisdom.[54] Again, they are . . .

> **Tradition**--a reading and remembering community (the church's legacy of biblical interpretation). There's no need to reinvent the wheel, although the past doesn't always have it exactly right. Even so, there is a body of important gathered wisdom waiting to be drawn upon. It always should be taken into consideration.
>
> **Reason**--testing for coherence of our best thoughts arising from all other wisdom now known. We Christians shouldn't park your brains at the church door but know that God's wisdom relates naturally to and can guide all other wisdom. Divine truth is logical and reasonable even if ultimately trans-rational.
>
> **Experience**--personally experiencing the impact of the divine revelation. Some things are only known well from the inside. Truth tends to be self-authenticating over time. We persons tend to know best the Person in intimate relationship with the Person.

What's most likely true? First, it's what the Bible says when interpreted with care. Then it's what has been reflected on carefully in light of what other believers have thought, and finally accepted only when it makes reasonable sense and tends to prove highly satisfying in our own lives as believing Bible readers.

We must not read the Bible disinterestedly, in isolation from our brothers and sisters in the faith. We must not seek truth with our brains disengaged, with our experiences not taken into account, or without personal relationship with the Spirit of truth. Truth tends to be clarified in the mixture of this perception pattern of checks and balances. It's the Quad that seeks to best honor God.

One contextual factor is crucial. Our whole process of Bible reading and interpreting is surrounded by the Spirit of God who *inspired* the Word initially and is anxious now to *illumine* its best understanding and application in present settings. God's Spirit always is present and prepared to work through each avenue of the Quad as they in turn interact with each other.

Here's a simple summary that seeks to order the complexity. The Bible is the preeminent norm of Christian truth. A responsible reading of its text necessarily involves interfacing with the church's past traditions, our most careful human reasoning, our present spiritual experience, and a faithful hearing of the voice of God's Spirit speaking to today's church.

The written witness to divine revelation, the Bible, relies for its best interpretation on a reading and remembering community, the process of existential appropriation, spiritual experience, employing a way to test for internal consistency, human reason, and honoring the wisdom of the Spirit who superintends the entire process. Knowing God's truth is a complex process. We are caught between ways of truth knowing. It's a captivity that offers true liberation.

Our challenge is to honor all these ways of knowing without ignoring any one and giving clear life evidence that all are taken seriously and leading to our making a positive difference in the world. It would be worth their reading an exceptional Quad man from seventeenth century France who is one of Christianity's best in this regard. There was a remarkable wholeness to Blaise Pascal's vision of truth.

Pascal's was the golden age of early modern science and a century of great religious revival. He was able to develop an integrated understanding of human experience focused on glorifying Jesus Christ. He never left behind his exceptional understanding of mathematics and science while discovering that thoroughgoing rationality is consistent with worship of the living God. One can come to know and love God with heart and mind. We believers can and must use that love and knowledge in the service of God.

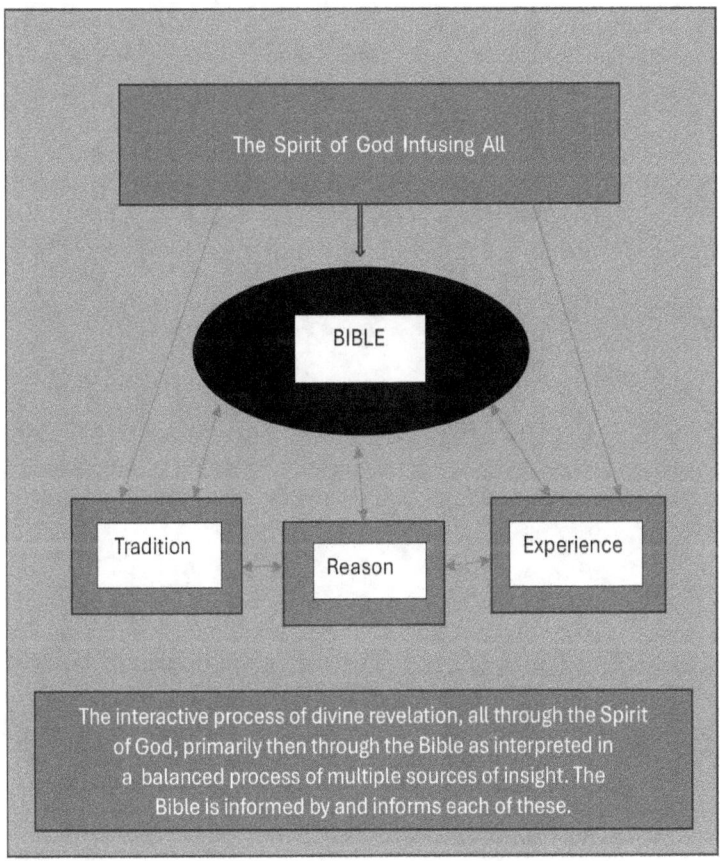

How easy it is for Christians to assume the divorce of heaven and earth. Many of us have unconsciously accepted a worldview that inverts the direction of salvation. We think salvation means only *going up to heaven* rather than also *heaven coming down to earth*.

The Bible teaches both. We have been taught that Jesus ascended to heaven so that our spirits could join him there eternally. That's wonderfully correct. So is this. God, as the Spirit of Jesus, is coming to earth to redeem all creation *now*.[55] Do you hear that call? Will you accept that challenge?

Chapter Eight

The Authority of Spiritual Experience

There will be scattered substance before there is ordered presentation. Ultimately, order is of importance, but there must be content before there is form. –Edgar Stranahan

It is by the Spirit alone that the true knowledge of God hath been, is, and can be revealed. And these revelations, which are absolutely necessary for the building up of true faith, neither do nor can ever contradict right reason or the testimony of the Scriptures. –John Wesley

No matter how sophisticated and compelling a Christian doctrine may sound, it first was a human experience or it has no real meaning. Only when Christian truth was experienced and shared by many others, mostly untheological people, was it formalized into concise theological language by specialists. Apart from experience, doctrines never would exist. They exist because something has happened that deserves explanation.

The original "theologians" of the Christian tradition were Hebrew, Greek, Roman, and North African, and since have been primarily European and North American, although increasingly supplemented by believers from other continents globally. Regardless of who or when such has happened, the truth in view always has had to be more than the result of an extensive rational exercise. The faith first had to be actually experienced and calling for formal expression so that it could be explained and shared with others.

A critical concern always is whether or not a religious "experience" necessarily involved anything more than the emotional power of the experience itself. "Myth" can be only an insightful story that somehow guides us through the thicket of thorns called life. A strong current in contemporary thought champions the idea of myth being disconnected from actual historical reality. We need to think again about this, and carefully. Christian faith assumes that its core experiences root in ultimate reality worthy of the fullest of possible explanations. It represents a *meta-narrative* representing the overarching story of God with us.

The testimony of some religious experiences can be "true" for the individual involved while not based on anything historically true otherwise. That is, "Jesus has become everything to me even if he never actually lived or at least was never really resurrected." Is "really happened" important? A recent survey asked people what was most important about their faith life. Only about forty percent said "the source of truth." It being the cause of some personal satisfaction was adequate for them.

The majority of people said things like "it brings comfort or emotional relief." Gained for them was not a new worldview, a fix on ultimate truth so much as a relaxation of personal tension, the release of guilt, the joy of being part of an accepting new community.[56] Such gains are of value, but hardly enough in the Christian view. "Good religion is more than some frothy tonic for our everyday neuroses."[57] It must have reality above and beyond us.

Christianity differs from many contemporary faith communities in that it's based on critical things believed to have really happened, things that alter our personal being *and* our understanding of what potentially is real for everyone at any time. Reason and emotion need kept in balance. "Conversion" for the Christian is an actual turning around of life that both spawns freedom and joy and provides a new perspective on the world of objective reality.

The joy comes from God's grace. God entices the life change through undeserved love. God loves so that change becomes possible and attractive. What empowers change, what makes one desirous of change is the experience of being loved and the undeserved acceptance it offers. Love is the engine of change.

There is an essential doubleness. Christian spiritual experience is to be an outgrowth of a related rational view of the reality that grounds the experience. Loss of either is a major loss indeed. The result would be doctrine with no real power or experience with nothing but subjective meaning for the person involved.

First Content, Then Form

If we consider seriously what the Bible says about the Holy Spirit, Bible study can be transformed from an intellectual struggle to a life-changing understanding, a relational event of knowing both the personal and trans-personal. In the Western world, we think of knowledge as a measurable thing. How much do you know about cars, computers, or chemistry? We think knowing requires observing, measuring, and categorizing. In the Bible, however, knowledge and wisdom are more relational processes than scientific outcomes.

The Bible in some ways is a post-modern book with an ancient Eastern origin. Biblical writers tended to "know" less by objective analysis and more by encountering a person or thing. Knowledge came through engagement. A cake was known less by studying the recipe and more by tasting a bite. Says Psalm 34:8, "taste and see." Sexual intimacy was really knowing a person. Knowledge arises out of shared experience.

The ancient Hebrews were less inclined to seek knowledge of the contents of a book than to know the author of the book as revealed by the contents. They meditated on the law of God less for self-improvement and more for knowing and pleasing the God they were coming to know. Wisdom was less knowing what to do in various circumstances and more knowing how to exist before God and with others in those circumstances.

In Christ, God is proclaimed to have come among us humans so that we might see and touch, truly know God by direct experience. The Bible's declaration is this. If we know Jesus in personal relationship, we know the Father. Knowing the Spirit of Jesus is the primary means of knowing Father and Son.

The Bible is an ancient book and also the present Word of God. It's living literature that transcends time because it's more than the words on the pages. Its goal is to guide readers to know God, not just come to know *about* God. Knowing God is not accomplished through reasoning alone. We know God through divine-human encounters by faith. Writers like Tolstoy and Dostoevsky bring Jesus to life because they approach him through the imagination as artists more than through the intellect as theologians.[58]

God is not speaking *at us* so much as *to us* with the desire to speak *with us,* and then even *through us* to others. God wants us to know, especially to know God's loving and restoring heart. Once knowing, we become ready to represent that knowing. Once experience is a reality, doctrinal expressions of that knowing can be attempted. They will be more time sensitive than the experiences. First is content and then form.

What is essential content for the Christian thinker? It's actual spiritual experience of new life in Jesus Christ. Before any intense intellectual exercise regarding Christian experience, there should come the experience itself. In the early church, the Spirit of God was an *encounter* before in human hands and minds it became a *doctrine*. Christian believers should not spend their precious time vigorously explaining and defending that which isn't personally known to them except abstractly in theoretical models of the mind. It's the experience of new life in the Spirit of God that makes one a true member of the church and a competent seeker after God's truth.

I admit to spending much time "doing theology," reviewing and writing freshly about the intellectual substance of Christian faith. But there is a major caution to be honored. Christian theology is not to be an independent exercise, rational activity for its own sake largely isolated from the real life of the church. Thinking deeply about the faith is essential, but hardly as an isolated ivory-tower priority. Abstract thinking is the task of philosophers. Theologians are to reflect in *form* what they already know in *experience.*

Jewish people already knew about God, at least in an historical and partial way. Then came to them a man who claimed to be God *actually with us*. Jesus was not the sort of man you could dismiss as a lunatic. He convinced many of those around him. They met him again after they had seen him brutally killed! Then, after they had been formed into a new faith community, they found God, the Spirit of Jesus, somehow inside them as well, directing them, making them able to do things they could not do before.

When the earliest Christian theologians had thought long and hard about all this, they finally arrived at a Christian definition of the Tri-Personal God. They were attempting to formulate in doctrine what they already knew by experience.[59] They now were thinking children of the Father, living in the Son, inspired and gifted by the Spirit.

Faith Seeking Understanding

A good theological guide involves a careful balancing of the Christ of *history* and the Christ of *experience*. Christianity is a faith with real historical roots that now function in the *present tense*.[60] The formalities of Christian teaching must be based on experienced religion. Christian theology is careful reflection on actual faith experience. Again, to do deep thinking about faith without any living of such faith is the business of philosophers and not theologians.

The primary goal of Christian faith is not to create a set of rationalized and precisely defined beliefs. Rather, it's to encounter a transforming relationship with God that fulfills life's intended meaning and destiny and inspires action in pursuing God's mission. God has not provided a highly-developed belief system or an eternal religious institution. Rather, we have been given access to life with the God now known most clearly in the person of Jesus Christ.

Christianity, then, is less a *religion* and more a faith *relationship*. It's more a trail of spiritual experiences that are life-changing and church building. The framing of beliefs is crucial, without question, but without substance and power if separated from the related experience.

Truth in its deepest meaning is available initially through a personal commitment to the divine love with which God first loved us. Once that redeeming love is known personally, the mind then can and should go into action seeking to better comprehend such an amazing reality. The task is to develop ways to frame experience so that it can be shared with and inspired in others. That's Christian experience theologically developed for evangelistic action, loving God with the whole mind on behalf of others. Theological expressions (creeds) are hardly final and not to be made mandatory except with considerable caution.

It's also reasonable to be cautious about relying on the legitimacy of spiritual experience for certainty in religious faith. Experience easily goes astray when on its own. Faith always will be required. Absolute certainty is an unreasonable hope for us limited humans. Reason must come into the picture as a check on the legitimacy and believability of claimed experience. Relative certainty can be achieved only when the Quad is faithfully employed.

John Wesley wisely considered Scripture to be God-inspired, trustworthy, the primary religious authority for Christian beliefs, values, and practices. However, he also appealed to tradition, reason, and experience as genuine and needful means of Christians reviewing, deepening, contextualizing, and finally proclaiming faith experiences. An analogy helps understanding of the integrative character of the Quad's operation.

Scripture, tradition, reason, and experience should function as an organic whole in the search to best understand and apply the revealed truth of God. Scripture serves as the head, but we should not speak of a single part of the body without reference to the wisdom contributions of the others. The various parts are necessarily interdependent in understanding the function of the whole.[61] Religious experience must be Spirit-directed, thought about carefully, enriched by the world of the church's rich memories, and enlivened by our own.

It's Time to Rebalance

The various dimensions of Chistian experience are to be seen in its worship patterns. Today the primary pattern may need some rebalancing for the sake of in-depth Christian understanding and integrity. Much Christian worship is being judged more popular performance than persuasive teaching of the great truths of the faith. Theological roots are quietly withering in some settings. Theater presentation threatens to overwhelm theological understanding.

People may be getting their felt needs well addressed, but possibly in ways encouraging considerable fallout for the church's future.[62] Christian worship should "quicken the conscience by the holiness of God, feed the mind with the truth of God, purge the imagination by the beauty of God, open the heart to the love of God, and devote the will to the purpose of God."[63] In other words, the worship of the

Christian community should honor the full range of the substance-style paradox that stimulates the deep knowing of believers.

It's common to experience in worship the clash of classic and contemporary, truth and entertainment, message and medium. Worship planners are caught between these tension-filled contrasts. Three types (styles) of worship music appear biblically recognized. All are encouraged, with a healthy congregation lacking none, no one emphasized over the others. Such balance addresses all elements of the Quad.

Colossians 3:16 says we believers are to worship "with gratitude in your hearts, sing psalms, hymns, and spiritual songs." Hymns are carefully crafted musical confessions about the nature and work of God. They are thoughtful and theological. Psalms are more memories of the ways God has worked in the many circumstances of the lives of past believers. Spiritual songs are current expressions of direct experiences of God's presence and grace. These musical types are the products of the faith's theologians, poets, and testifiers, with the differing emphases of mind, memory, and emotion. All are valuable and very much belong.

Hymns are foundational, biblically grounded, and thoughtfully stated. The others music types are increasingly devotional and emotionally expressive of experiences with this rich theological grounding. Without the first, worship becomes self-centered and misguided. Without the relational richness of the second and third, worship tends to become impersonal, lacking the joyous and expressive wisdom of the immediacy of the moment.

A healthy congregation needs the songs of the Bible, the songs of the ages, and the songs of the moment. It needs songs that express the soul, reflect on memories, stretch the mind, and rejoice the heart. It needs Bible songs, hymnbook songs, and chorus songs. Songs of theology without the underlying spiritual experience excite no one. Songs of experience without theological understanding can be more passing emotion that enduring commitment that's well understood. All are very much needed.

In many worship settings, it appears time to think again. There's much clapping and dancing and loud sound and a lack of in-depth teaching to ground the emotion with understanding. A hymn is not just an old song that earlier generations composed and relished. It can be a new composition like "In Christ Alone" composed in 2001 by Getty and Townsend in the United Kingdom. These lyrics retell the core biblical story of God in Christ for our salvation, with the music quite singable by the typical congregation.

Theology can be sung in a few verses as well as written in large books with specialized language unknown to the average believer. It should find its way into all experiences of worship so that believers are constantly exposed to biblical revelation presented with care and compassion for the searching mind and the struggling soul.

Churches also need songs of personal and immediate religious experience, especially when they are well supported by the theological substance that keeps them in perspective. Worship music should teach and testify to the faith. Today we need a rebalancing. Post-moderns still want the reasonable and defensible. They also want real community gathered around experience that gives life to the immediate setting.

There is to be the "orthodox" and the "charismatic." Orthodox means straight thinking while charismatic means gifted experiencing and sacrificial living based on that thinking. One holds and teaches correctly the ideas of the faith while the other relishes and employs the gifts of the Spirit for the good of the fellowship and the world. One remembers and understands well while the other springs freshly out of the precious memories and celebrates well.

One has traditional position in the faith community and the other focuses freshly on the current presence of the Spirit who constitutes the community and inflames its mission. The first can be right and yet not experienced as real. The second can be emotionally exciting and yet theologically erratic and unacceptable. True church life flourishes in the proper combination of clear thinking that is alive with essential emotion and action rooted in such thinking.

Time to Experience--Thoughtfully

It's time to think *spiritually* and experience the spiritual *thoughtfully*. This key and yet delicate complexity protects against mere rationalism and emotional self-delusion. People must become dissatisfied with anything less than careful thinking about the Christian faith that necessarily proceeds to be couched in the transformation of a new *Pentecost*. Ponder these inspired words:

> Thou, who's purpose is to kindle:
> Now ignite us with Thy fire;
> While the earth awaits Thy burning,
> With Thy passion us inspire.
> Overcome our sinful calmness,
> Rouse us with redemptive shame;
> Baptize with Thy fiery Spirit,
> Crown our lives with tongues of flame.[64]

Being tough-minded and warm-hearted is admittedly a demanding balancing act. Even so, the personal experience of Pentecost is essential, even primary for the real Christian in today's world. We must hear the twin biblical calls to love God with all our minds and to meditate day and night on God's law (Ps 1:1). We are to be prepared to give thoughtful reasons for the hope that is within us (1 Pet 3:15) and be experiencing new life in the Spirit that brings such hope.

John Wesley modeled well this core duality. The best Christian theologian is not one lost in the books. It's the *pastor-theologian* who is actively thinking and teaching and also shepherding Christian disciples as they engage the world.[65]

Be warned. No matter how important spiritual experience is, it can be as undependable as essential. Intense transformative experiencers are the church's lifeblood, and also some of its biggest problems. A believer can be so lifted into another world that there is little relevance shown for this one. A believer constantly on knees with visions from above can be naïve and complacent about institutional and sociological realities and responsibilities all around.

There are numerous examples of emotional and poorly informed believers "falling prey to bizarre apocalyptic, dispensational, or millennial views which are unbiblical and unrealistic and may lead to extreme hopes, claims, or behavior."[66] Sound biblical interpretation must accompany the trans-rational divine dimension of Christian experience. Being on one's knees occasionally is the only way to stand properly. Even so, staying on one's knees is not the best posture for facing courageously the world's great challenges.

Bible study must be more than flashes of spiritual excitement. Interpreting it cannot be irrational, bypassing human understanding and reason. Still, through the Holy Spirit, Bible study can transcend human reason without violating it. We are gifted from above to really know, even if always knowing only in part.

The ministry of the Holy Spirit transcends our reason, granting discernment, knowledge, wisdom and understanding beyond our natural abilities. The Spirit flows in ways we cannot dictate. By the Spirit, we can *know* more than we can *understand*.

Bible study empowered by the Holy Spirit enriches reason without bypassing it. We come to know the Word of God with knowledge that is of the Spirit. We are to study hard, apply ourselves, God gladly receiving our efforts as an offering. The Spirit then adds to this offering necessary gifts of grace.

We must come to see the truth, know the truth, embrace the truth, and then be enabled to be changed and begin to relate and serve by the truth. We then will begin to understand what Augustine meant when, in his *Answer to Skeptics*, he announced that the study of God requires intellectual effort, historical imagination, empathic energy, and participation in a vital community of prayer.

The call often heard is "Back to the Blessed Old Bible," thought the best way of finding our way back to God. This goal is most worthy, although requiring more than merely reading the book itself. It means reading in a way that stimulates encountering and being reformed in the image of the One who through this book can become known to us as the gracious Author of all things! When the Bible is read only "objectively," looking for bits of wise religious information without personal relationship to God, it's read falsely and will not yield its best treasures.

The focus on human reason, while clearly having its advantages, tends to reduce the Bible to a series of words, ideas, beliefs, and propositions that can be researched with a computer program and managed with our human minds. The result is a depersonalizing of the text, turning it into pressing questions and supposed answers, definitions and dogmas we can memorize, repeat, put on a spreadsheet and use for personal purposes. But the Bible is intended to be something else, something more, much more.

The Bible has no independent existence as divine revelation apart from the present ministry of the Spirit who originally inspired it. If we try to manage it as a stand-alone artifact of ancient times now waiting for our rational analysis, or if we see it as a free-standing self-help guide for life in modern times that we can apply at will, the Bible will be a dead letter in our hands.

To read this sacred book as God wishes requires coming to know God personally and listening to the divine voice that always seeks to emerge from within the written text. Relating to and responding to this voice is the proper way to probe the in-depth meaning of the words. The best listening is done in community, the church, and not alone.

Yesterday's divine *inspiration* of the Bible intends to move to today's divine *illumination*. Bible reading must be more than the transference of helpful historic and religious information. It's primarily to be a guide for our journey into the mysterious and marvelous past and current presence and mission of God. It seeks to manage us more than we managing it.

The biblical text should be removed from the hands of self-oriented "modernity" where it's been reduced to an object to be bought, sold, and even used as a weapon. Such tragic reduction has happened in both Christian "liberalism" and "fundamentalism." Each has defensively reduced the biblical text to its "factual essence" that can be handled as desired by us over-confident contemporary readers. Liberalism highlights human ideals overlaid on the biblical text.

Fundamentalism chooses an isolated chunk of a biblical text pulled from the parent narrative and forces it into support a foreign agenda. It relies on a literalist style of Bible reading. But "literalism is the lowest and least level of meaning in a spiritual text. Willful people use Scripture literally when it serves their purposes and figuratively when it gets in the way of their cultural biases. Willing people let the Scriptures change *them* instead of using them to change *others*."[67]

To know God is the path to becoming more like God. Reading the Bible with the intention of coming to know and be changed by God brings the possibility of mysteriously becoming a new participant in the divine life. Reading rightly the book of God means allowing

God to read and transform us as we read. "Spiritual" Bible reading seeks to get beyond rote religious concepts and imposed belief systems to present life change. The pages of the Word remain the vehicle of the persistent Presence, the Spirit-Word seeking to transform every reader into an "icon" of that Presence.

To be "Christian" is to be a person re-formed in the image and reflective of the love of Jesus. Bible reading is to serve this re-formation by guiding us into becoming "holy as God is holy." This "sanctifying" process is mysterious, amazing, available, and much too uncommon. It seeks to separate us from the sins of today's culture and send us into that culture with the loving power of its possible transformation.

The Bible is a *transparency* leading to God God more than an encyclopedia of religious information. Given the language, culture, timing, and literary-style issues that complicate interpretation of all ancient documents, the Bible included, we believers should come to the biblical text looking less for what we think we can see *in it* and more what we are helped by God to see and encounter *through it.* Our eyes are to be enabled to see the Father acting in the Son, resurrection life present beyond sin and death, and eternal blessedness overcoming today's suffering and unanswered questions.

True disciples of Jesus are Pentecost people in whom the Spirit reveals the Son as our way to the Father, to our renewed ourselves, and to each other. We are to do *Spirit-Word* biblical reading, being intentional about opening ourselves to the Bible's divine presence, insight, and power. This is "re-enchanting" the biblical text.[68] It moves beyond the words to encounters with the *Presence* who is the foundation and final interpreter of the present meaning of all biblical words. Truth is personal relationship and transformation. It's "Christ in you—the hope of glory" (Col 1:27).

The way to read the Bible is to know Jesus as now alive in the ministry of the Spirit and to hear God's voice speaking through the biblical text for the purpose of present transformation of people and societies. We must let go of fixations on previous ideas, doctrines, and religious institutions. Required is releasing ourselves to the present understandings and mission of the Spirit.

The Word Above the Language

Our minds and hearts now must explore the divinely infused words of the Bible without counseling others "by words without knowledge" (Job 38:2). We never should twist biblical words for private purposes, justifying ourselves (Job 40:8) and dishonoring God with proclamations of our own ignorance. Bible words are to be handled humbly as conveyances of divine truths that transcend the words. Full understanding will be Spirit-assisted. This is impossible apart from actually being alive in Christ.

The proper approach to reading biblical materials should reflect Job's final answer back to God. "I'm speechless, in awe, words fail me. I should never have opened my mouth. I've talked too much, way too much. I'm ready to shut up *and listen*" (40:3-5, *The Message*). The entire biblical text is to be approached this way, openly, with more questions than pre-conceived answers, with the focus on being in touch with God more than reaching for air-tight answers to current questions.

Leo, Bishop of Rome, said that "Christ became the Son of Man so that we could become children of God." Regarding Christmas, he called on us "to think of the Lord's birth, wherein the Word became flesh, not as a past event which we recall but as a present reality upon which we gaze." That's needed wisdom for today's Bible reading. We are to gaze patiently at the mystery of the ages, Jesus Christ, until we realize that God still is reaching in love for us and all others. Yesterday's incarnation in Jesus Christ is to be today's incarnation of the Spirit in us!

The truth of biblical revelation is always more than can be read with human eyes and analyzed with human brains. The text carries an eternal *more*. Job reached the higher goal, the necessary more, *the actual Presence of God*. "I had heard of you by the hearing of the ear, but now mine eyes *see you*" (42:5). Seeing the Divine is preparation for understanding properly the inspired Word of God. Herein lies true spiritual authority.

Chapter Nine

A Solid Place To Stand

Give me a place to stand and I will move the earth. –Archimedes.

I shall be entitled to entertain the highest expectations if I am fortunate enough to discover only one thing that is certain and indubitable. –Rene Descartes

Jesus offers himself as God's doorway into the life that is truly life (Jn 6). Confidence in him leads us today, as in other times, to become his apprentices in eternal living. –Dallas Willard

---

The last chapter stressed the potential authority lodged in authentic Christian "experience." Now we address the balancing factor. For the Christian, truth is to be more than our experience of it. What's actually believed to be real must go beyond strong feelings to careful thinking about something solid, substantially real and unmovable. That's necessary to communicate effectively with postmoderns who aren't sure that there is anything unmovable.

We now must get beyond the ancient Chinese Taoist philosophy of achieving life's ultimate goal by finding "Tao," the Way. What is this Way? One journalist described it as trying to hug a seal covered with slick lotion. It's something hard to get hold of, indescribable, known only when gained, the quiet place of the *Yin-Yang*.

The Way is said to be the benevolent force that flows through all things, the deep way things ought to be when they become what they ought to be. If this isn't clear, it's because *it isn't*. That's just the mysterious manner by which things are to be resolved according to this idealistic and contentless Taoist faith tradition.

A word defining well the circumstance today is *confusion*. People don't know what to think, or even whether thinking is what they should be doing. The resulting spiritual emptiness and lostness of life is a dangerous situation in which any new dogmatism may arise. If, according to post-modernism, all "truth" is likely only a product of some community's inside thinking, then Christianity and all faith communities stand on slippery ground, especially when trying to evangelize others.

The historic base of Christian faith is very specific and has been judged true inside and outside this faith community. It claims that a particular human life, Jesus, once really appeared within a marginalized culture during a distant time in human history. The first Christians thought clearly and dramatically about this appearance. They believed that Jesus, a real man among us humans, held within himself "all the treasures of wisdom and knowledge" (Col 2:3) for all humans in all times.

This confidence in the unequaled significance of Jesus is the radicalism of any who dare to be followers of Christ today. We join their sisters and brothers of long ago in seeing Jesus now living beyond death as "the faithful witness, the first born of the dead, the ruler of the kings of the earth, the first and the last, the living One who can properly say, 'I was dead, and behold, I am alive, forevermore, the master of death and the world of the dead'" (Rev 1:5, 18).

Such a bold statement would make Jesus a solid place to stand when determining truth. Therefore, it's time to think again about who really is a "Christian." Is it enough to be a member of a Christian family or a formal member of a Christian church? What about having been "saved" by accepting God's forgiveness for past sin? Does that make one an instant Christian? Yes, in an important sense, but no in another important sense.

Here's a clear definition. A Christian is a person who becomes convinced that the fact of Jesus Christ is the most trustworthy fact known in any time or setting, and because of this belief dedicates all of life to existence in light of and on behalf of this amazing fact. There is one, and only one, Jesus, who has broken through the solid wall of "only the here and now, only for our group" and is the ultimate of what always was and ever will be for all people everywhere.

To be a Christian in this sense is a daring stance in today's postmodern culture with all its relativisms. It involves believing deeply that Jesus is God's doorway into the life that truly is life (Jn 6). He alone is *God with us*, the singular path to our salvation! This dramatic exclusivism runs against the grain of today's general thought. Therefore, it must be thought about very carefully and lived out credibly if there is hope of its intended impact.

The Only Fully Trustworthy One

I'll make the dramatic statement again. A Christian is a person who confesses that, amid the many confusing voices heard in the world, there is one alone who deserves our full belief. That voice is Jesus Christ, judged the one truly stable point in all the relativities of human history. A person who realizes this and seeks to align with it "begins to know the joy of being used for a mighty purpose by which life is dignified."[69]

When encountering Jesus and his claims about himself, either we have to reject him as another overly arrogant false prophet or accept him *on his own terms*. If Jesus is right, then there is a solid place to stand, a perspective that brings all else into focus. Jesus offers a stable place to stand in the midst of the world's confusion.

Consider the significance of the prayer of Jesus (Matt 11:25, Lk 10:21). "I thank Thee, Father, Lord of heaven and earth, that you have hidden these things from the wise and revealed them to babies." Here is an entire theology by which people can live, one compatible with the best of rationality while extending beyond the knowing capability of mere humans. "Once accepting the conviction of the Christlikeness of God, we have a firm launching pad from which we can operate with confidence and make a consequent difference in the world."[70]

Listen to the critical announcement Malcolm Muggeridge. "We all know how increasingly hollow and unconvincing it is--the great society, mankind coming of age, men like gods, all the unspeakable fantasies of utopians on the run. As far as I am concerned, the only solution is Christ. I have failed to find in past experience, present dilemmas, or future expectations any alternative proposition."[71]

The result of accepting such a grand proposition is hardly simplistic, but neither is it necessarily out of reach. Its complexity is crucial but not crippling. Granted, we humans cannot *comprehend* ultimate truth in any final and controlling sense, but by the sheer grace of God we may be enabled to *apprehend* it to an adequate and satisfying degree. The following haunting line is found in the song *"Understanding Nothing"* by Bruce Cockburn. "All these years of thinking ended up like this. In front of all this beauty, understanding nothing." How pathetic, ironic, sad, and possibly unnecessary!

The call to Christian believers is to embrace relative "ignorance," admitting that we humans know little for sure. Even so, in great humility we can believe that there stands before us Jesus, the needed fulcrum of all wisdom. The ultimate in life is not a math problem to be solved but a *Person* seeking relationship with us. It then comes down to our willingness to stand in awe, unsure, and yet by faith quite sure of words like "amazing grace."

We find ourselves pondering in our unknowing a reasonable faith. We find ourselves rejoicing in the known presence of the fullness of truth. Our feet search desperately for a sturdy foothold before we stumble into the abyss. They catch on something that doesn't move, that stabilizes, that saves. His name if Jesus.

What has happened to enable this finding? We have caught a glimpse of God who is known fully in Jesus Christ. What we need aren't final answers to all difficult life questions so much as an unmovable Rock on which to stand while some questions remain unanswered. Here's the good news.

> We have an Anchor that keeps the soul,
> Steadfast and sure while the billows roll.
> Fastened to the Rock which cannot move,
> Grounded firm and deep in the Savior's love.[72]

Finding Christ gives stability for facing the questions and challenges of life. Jesus found himself in the wilderness and yet withstood the enemy by knowing how to distinguish the voices pulling at him. We believers find ourselves in the wilderness of today's world and need not be lost or defeated if we can distinguish among the voices and hear the only one that is authentic.

Thomas Merton once pondered prayerfully the awkward experience of being in the wilderness with God. He found himself praying like this.

> My Lord God, I have no idea where I am going. I do not see the road ahead of me. I cannot know for certain where it will end. But I believe that the desire to please you does, in fact, please you. And I know that you will lead me by the right road although I may know nothing about it. Therefore, I will trust you always though I may seem to be lost and in the shadow of death. I will not fear for you are ever with me, and you will never leave me alone in the face of my perils.[73]

Such is the assurance of God's stabilizing voice. "Fear not for I am with you, I am your God, I will strengthen you and uphold you with my righteous right hand" (Isa 41:10). Said Jesus, "I am with you always to the very end of the age" (Matt 28:20). In this truth-enlightening presence, in the rich arena of the Person-to-person relationship with Jesus, troubling dilemmas have a way of melting into satisfying paradoxes that manage to grasp the whole of complex truths and be satisfied.

To be Christian is to receive gratefully the full truth of Jesus Christ. Sometimes our human thinking can't find its way to all desired answers. Faith requires that we rest in this paradoxical circumstance. It's knowing and not knowing, believing in the *who* of Jesus while having to proceed on our faith journey despite lack of clarity about the *what's* behind detailed doctrines and competing faiths. The complexity of Christian truth requires an ongoing journey beyond any simple rational process.

Christian faith doesn't try to solve all the mysteries of faith. We are dealing with God and God with us in Jesus. Solving the divine mysteries with mental simplicities is likely to fall into the muddy world of heresy. Encountering the mysteries of God calls for humbly being in touch, but without full possession of the ultimate truth itself.

Rather than providing all answers, perceiving God through Jesus Christ presents at least the proper angle of view and spawns exhilaration and wonder if not always final answers. It's a solid place to stand, building our homes on the rock and not on shifting sand.

Here's biblical wisdom. "We are human pilgrims following the pathways of knowledge. To the end of the earthly way, we shall know only in part. Even so, our faith in Jesus Christ can give us the assurance of things hoped for and the conviction of things not seen."[74] It's quite a claim to make for a baby born in a barn to very poor parents.

Little Jesus was both fully human and fully divine, destined to be crucified by the humans of his own creation. Why? Because to them he was unrecognized, unacceptable, although the loving heart of his Father in action on their behalf! Knowing this is somehow to know everything of value, to have a solid place to stand.

Descartes may have been wrong about some things, but not this. "I shall be entitled to entertain the highest expectations if I am fortunate enough to discover only one thing that is certain and indubitable." David Elton Trueblood announces his big discovery in *A Place To Stand*. The New Testament proclamation is that we humans are fortunate indeed. There really is good news in the face of which the whole creation trembles. *His name is Jesus!*

A pilot was practicing high-speed maneuvers in a jet fighter. She turned the controls for what she thought was a steep ascent and flew straight into the ground, unaware that she had been flying upside down. Is this a parable of human existence in our times?

Most of us are living at high-speed, and often with no clue as to whether we are flying upside down or right side up. Even worse, there is the haunting suspicion that maybe there's no difference in which way we fly. We're going nowhere with no flight plan anyway and a final crashing is inevitable. If only we were sure of how to reach the sky![75]

God's desire is that we be on steady course upward, living in and for the divine. God has sent among us the Way to himself. It's the needed orienting way that shows God's true heart of hearts, what reality is really like, which direction is up. Our universe is a community of boundless and competent love. Its intention is life in light of Jesus. It's a dying to death and living by the power of Life itself.

Jesus is the Bread of life that offers the doorway to the nourished life as we become his apprentices in eternal living. With arrival in baby Jesus, God "set afoot a conspiracy of freedom in truth among human beings. By relying on his word and presence, we are enabled to re-integrate the little realm that makes up our life into the infinite rule of God."[76]

This is clear and critical Christian thinking for our day. The historic revelation of Christ gives solid footing; the revelation of the Holy Spirit in each contemporary life gives universality; and it's the combination of these that makes vital Christianity possible for all.

Knowing Doctrine in Depth

Here's an idea needing thought again. Christian faith is much more than religious ideas. It's intensely *relational*, persons actually being related to Jesus and living in his transforming presence. Real knowing is hardly limited to our faith hearing what Christ said long ago and trying to carry it out today. Rather, "The real Son of God is at your side. He is beginning to turn you into the same kind of thing as Himself. He is beginning, so to speak, to 'inject' His kind of life and thought, His *zoe* [life], into you; beginning to turn the tin soldier into a live man. The part of you that does not like it is the part that is still tin."[77]

Dallas Willard lived as a child where electricity was available only as lightning. Then the Rural Electrification Administration extended its lines into that area of Missouri, bringing a very different way of living. Amazing new power changed many things about daily life. Similarly, being infused by the presence of the kingdom of God come near in Jesus brings a fundamental change of life itself. Knowing in depth in light of Jesus produces fresh life to the full.

The Christian good news is that there has arrived in our part of the world an eternal "lightning" from above. It shines and brings to life a present reality that can alter all of life. What happened in the past can be happening in our personal present.

The Pentecost event reported in the Book of Acts provides the connecting link between the past of Christian beginnings and the present of our Christian beginnings. It's the continuity between the historic presence of Jesus and our present salvation. Such is realized when one lives in intimate relationship to Jesus through his Spirit.

Christian faith is not simply about *knowing* the truth in Christ. It also is about being *transformed* by that truth into a person mirroring it and acting as its agent by the "power of God now available for our salvation" (Rom 1:16). The New Testament intends to aid readers to be faithful to the contemporary meaning of Jesus. The Bible is the book of the Spirit to be interpreted in light of God's Self-revelation in Jesus Christ as the Spirit guides now in grasping the meaning of Jesus for ourselves and our time.

We cannot keep the Law of God by merely trying hard to do it. We must aim at something more than a successful moral achiever. We must become the kind of persons from whom the deeds of the Law naturally flow. This is key to understanding the "Sermon on the Mount" of Jesus. He constantly contrasts the mistake of the Scribes and Pharisees with his disciples living a new life of love *in light of himself*.

The Scribes and Pharisees focused on the actions that the Law required and insisted on detailed conformity of action. They were self-conscious about doing all the right things while Jesus was calling for something else, new lives of love that naturally fulfill the intent of the Law. He said that an adequate fulfilling of the Law of God comes from practicing the *law of love*.

Christian doctrines and creeds seek to formulate in verbal packages divine truth as understood in light of Christ. Always is a degree of inadequacy to these packages. A life hidden with God could be likened to falling in love. Theological statements come along to package understandings of this love. However, any essay on love and actually being in love are not quite the same thing even if about the same thing.

Being in a love relationship with God is more foundational and fulfilling than a few faltering words trying to describe adequately this experience. There's a world of difference between learning to repeat "God is an omnipotent being" and addressing God directly with "Thou art *my* God!"

Christian faith and life doesn't begin with an academic thesis discovered in the mind but with a love relationship initiated by God. Believers should first seek to love the Lord as known in Jesus and then put that life-transforming love experience into words the best way possible for the understanding of others.

We should seek forgiveness whenever we insist that others word their beliefs exactly the way we have. We should focus more on the love relationship and less on frail theological formality. Our creeds are constructive means of sharing the faith and not clubs to gain and maintain dominance of our own thinking.

The Real God

The central truth of Christian theology is the particular nature and intention of God now shown to us by Jesus. God created humans with the ability to choose the intended good. God's great love accepts our decisions and is open to participating constructively in the suffering created by the evil of our wrong choices.

A key characteristic of God's nature is quite other than what many expect. God's exhibits a voluntary vulnerability on our behalf. Our ability to choose is a gift of God, a "risk" God willingly and lovingly has taken. Divine love and vulnerability are seen most clearly in a Bethlehem barn and on a cross just outside Jerusalem. God with us died for us!

The resurrection of Jesus makes dramatically plain that God was *with us* and *for us* as the Son murdered on the cross and now reigning in glory. Mystery remains, as does the awe of such amazing grace. What we do know is that darkness has been overwhelmed by light. Given the resurrection of Jesus, even that ugly cross now glows with glory. The heart of biblical revelation is this. God in Christ has identified personally, at great cost, and transformingly with our sin and suffering.

The main answer to our sin problem is the pain of God, voluntary divine participation in our suffering, the innocent for the guilty. Through unmerited love, our guilt can be purged of divine judgment and cleansed of its continuing power over our existence and destiny. That's the heart of all good Christian theology. It comes before doctrines that try to capture such grand meanings in a few theological words.

Good theology always moves between two poles, the Bible as the primary narrative source and the present culture with its distinctive mental categories and language. Scripture remains the narrated norm while effective communication demands doctrinal thought forms of the present time and place.[78] Our expressions should be confident but not cocky, personal witness but not frontal attack on the sincere expressions of others.

Faith is the victory that overcomes the world. Sometimes we wrongly say that doubt is faith's chief enemy. Still, all of us who believe experience times of doubt unless we live in a state of denial or a thoughtless void. Faith can falter when suffering surges. We all have a stake in the ancient prayer, "Lord I believe, help my unbelief" (Mk 9:24).

A real advance in the life of faith awaits believers who develop a more realistic attitude toward doubt. There may be more genuine faith in honest doubt than in blindly believing some conventional creed. Doubt keeps faith awake and moving. It isn't so much the opposite of faith as an agent of its refinement. We always, however, should dare to doubt *even our doubts*.

A great word of biblical faith is "nevertheless!" Our generalizations can be contradicted and our dogmas dynamited by evil life events. Still, these disruptions don't deserve the last word. Beyond them should come the persistent faith assertion, "nevertheless!" The Greek *ginosko* means "to know." When you put the prefix *epi* in front, it gets intensified into *really knowing*. That's what we want, to truly perceive, to know intimately, not just intellectually but in a way that alters life itself and survives life's ups and downs (1 Cor 13:12; 2 Pet 1:8).

The two men on their way to Emmaus met and talked with a stranger, the resurrected Jesus. Then "their eyes were opened and they recognized him" (Lk 24:31). They moved from knowing to *really knowing*. Faith has eyes that see beyond the obvious and immediate. The sturdiest survival rests in the lap of a matured relationship with Jesus, not merely in thinking about standard doctrines that seek to define him.

The theological works of John Wesley and Clark Pinnock are quite nuanced and yet not designed for intellectual elites. These were "practical" theologians deeply concerned about church renewal, partly through the established "means of grace," and sometimes by unexpected manifestations of God's Spirit.

The Spirit of Jesus can render common material things agents of spiritual insight and growth. Some of these just seem to happen as individuals are open to the Spirit's presence and revealing intent. Material carriers of the Spirit's truth and life are called "icons." Have there been any in your life recently? Stroke a baby, watch a sunset, feed the hungry, inhale the fragrance of a flower and be touched by God. When you are touched, what you have seen and done can become agents that open the eyes of your heart to God's presence and working.

From West to East

The Schism of 1054 divided the Western and Eastern worlds of Christianity. The great mysteries of the faith, like the doctrine of God, are approached rather differently in these still divided worlds. The West, Roman Catholicism and most of Protestantism, tends toward theological *analysis* while the East favors the worship of pure *adoration*.

There are major Western "systematic" theologies, like those of Aquinas, Calvin, Barth, and many others. Such are rarely found in the East. Christian leaders there are more comfortable in merging reason and experience, theology and spirituality, the mysteries of iconic cognition not needing to be resolved by carefully crafted human language.

John Wesley is something of an exception in the West. Rather than speculating at length about complex philosophic concepts, he joined the East in focusing on holiness, a theological understanding and relationship goal centering in actually communing with the living God.

Especially with his brother Charles, the great Christian hymn writer, John recognized the value of music and community dynamics in the quest for truth and the maturing faith of personal transformation. Aesthetic images and testimonies of spiritual experience are highlighted in addition to classic documents and complex arguments. John was a "practical" theologian.

Serious believers in Jesus tend to be caught in a tension. It's a pull to the left and to the right, creating the urgent need to be solidly anchored in the middle. Paradoxically, often we are caught between truths. Jointly required is a strong theological foundation and a robust world mission. We are to be both profoundly conservative in our anchored identity and passionately active in our missional engagement.

Put otherwise, we are to be middle-way and on-the-move disciples who know the Christ and are becoming like Christ (sanctification) and being Christ to others. This doesn't mean being compromised in some muddled middle accommodation. We are to be both anchored and stretching, believing even while exploring, going on without losing our roots.[79] The Spirit will help us become better in our thinking and stronger in our acting as we engage in the fray of our own becoming participants in the divine life. We must walk with the Spirit and grow as we go.

A friend was teaching his daughter to drive. It came time to try one of the freeways in California, and that meant approaching the first cloverleaf, a long and sweeping 270° curve. She experienced fear and did her share of jerking the car in constant corrections. Her father advised, "Don't look at the outside edge of the curve. Fix your eyes on the inside edge and stay close."[80]

In Christian faith, it's best to be center-focused and not looking at the boundaries and being confused about the center. Stay fixed on Christ, the solid place to stand and always the orienting place to look.

Chapter Ten

The Company of the Committed

> It is impossible for persons to meet with God and love God without at the same time meeting with and loving one another. –Jon Baillie

> The image guiding Christian presence in the world is not one of sovereignty, whereby we should increasingly bring it about that the world should be ruled by believers or by their ideas, but one of servanthood. – John Howard Yoder

Christianity is social by nature. It's hard to be Christian alone, nearly impossible. Once Christ is known in a heart, that knowledge tends to find or produce a fellowship to which we can belong and in which the living Christ is the head. Membership and unity in the fellowship of Christ should arise from a mutual sense of the power of Christ transforming each individual and then gifting each for the good of the larger whole.

The church is key to Christian life and mission. When gathered, the church is more than an audience of believers coming to hear a speaker or participate in a set of standard religious ceremonies. The truly Christian community is one in which all members "have unlimited liability for one another."[81] All are called to be "saints" *together*.

Holiness should mark all maturing members as the Spirit of God works to restore the image of Christ in each as preparation for all to minister in the world. To be holy may seem an impossible goal, but it's the goal of the Spirit in church life, the one to be achieved together on behalf of others.[82] It's only possible sacrificially and corporately. To fail to be like God (holy) is to fail to represent God believably in the world.

It's best to think of the church as *gathered* more than *given*. Being gathered speaks of the dynamic and voluntary. Given speaks more of something established, institutionalized with its accumulated order and standardized practices. Gathered suggests a living body responding to Christ, an instrument in the Spirit's hands. Given tempts to yield to human domination.[83] One is the company of the committed, the other more a club of members with common interests. It's time to think seriously about the importance of this fundamental distinction.

Complacent Religious Societies

The church, the universal body of Jesus people, has huge potential for good. It is rich in gifted personnel and well-meaning programs of good news capable of addressing a wide range of human sins and hurts. The church also is a paradox. With all this potential, it also experiences frequent frustrations that sideline its effectiveness. A prominent Christian brother once admitted this. "Sometimes I feel as though the church as it actually exists is the source of all my doubts and difficulties."[84]

Current cultural thinking is hard on community thinking, including the community of the church. The marketplace of our everyday life is designed to motivate choosing the products it offers to meet our private preferences. Community tends to be thought of as little more than a collection of individuals that exists for the need fulfillment of its individual members.

Phrases like "body of Christ" and "people of God" have lost much of their biblical meanings. The church has become a voluntary collection of individuals choosing to be present because a particular place, personality, or program is thought to meet best their perceived personal needs and desires. If that practical relevance changes, they are soon gone to the brighter lights and better music of elsewhere.

Concern for the transforming effectiveness of the church evolved over the years for Elton Trueblood. The maturing can be seen in his books *The Company of the Committed* and *The Incendiary Fellowship*. Always pleased to announce that he was a lifelong member of the Religious Society of Friends (Quakers), he once admitted that he accepted unconditionally this dictum of Samuel Taylor Coleridge.

"He who begins by loving Christianity better than truth will proceed by loving his own sect or church better than Christianity, and end in loving himself better than all."

We always must approach the established church with high expectation and definite caution. Many believers in Jesus now are looking for a bold fellowship and too often are finding complacent religious societies absorbed with their own internal politics and expansion desires. Congregations become unimaginative by assuming that the world can be saved by three hymns and a sermon or a mass on Sunday morning, and without the world present or knowing anything about all this inside stuff.

In fact, the primary purpose of a Christian fellowship is *evangelistic*. We believers are to live and breathe *for others*. The church of Jesus is really itself only when continually drawing outsiders into the incendiary circle of God's Spirit where they become so excited that soon they find themselves reaching out to ignite others.

The problem faced by the church today often is not so much lack of belief. It's that millions who do believe have no sense of urgency about the Christian endeavor in the world. They represent the difference between believing *that* (mental exercise) and believing *in* (personal commitment). Their believing doesn't include being fully invested in the relevance and mission of their belief.

Believing *in* must mean that all of oneself is impacted and becomes fully engaged. Such commitment will be widely effective only when it finds expression in a committed fellowship of like-minded and like-motivated believers. Such a fellowship is the church that Jesus had in mind. He instructed his first disciples to wait before launching their mission for him. Why wait? They needed igniting by the Spirit before facing a hostile world.

The advantage of believing *in* the reality of the divine Trinity, for instance, "is not that we get an 'A' from God for giving the right answer. To really believe something is to *act as if it is so*. The church is gathered to live as if the Trinity is real, as if the whole cosmos actually is a community of unspeakably magnificent personal beings of boundless love, knowledge, and power and, thus believing, lives naturally integrate themselves through our actions into the reality of such a universe."[85] That's church thinking and mission sending. It's time to think like this again!

The urgent question is how the church of Jesus Christ today can be reconstructed in order to play its intended role in the redemption of contemporary civilization. An ideal place to begin is a radical reappraisal of the amazing vitality of the early Christian church. Every thoughtful person should be deeply moved when considering the victory of the early church against apparently insurmountable odds. Initially, the church was only a band of dejected fishermen and 120 nervous and poorly-informed people gathered in an upper room in Jerusalem. That motley Jesus movement seemed likely to collapse quickly under the weight of its own insignificance.

However, it didn't collapse. It went from weakness to strength and not only survived but soon provided the center of an enduring civilization when the dominance of Greece and Rome faded. This was completely unexpected and highly unlikely. Amazing! Something about this dramatic fact reveals the true pattern of the intended Christian movement for our day. It's time to think carefully in order to discover this divine dynamic of growth and social impact.

The call of Jesus to "follow me" was hardly his advising people to go to church on Sunday morning. Instead, he was gathering "recruits in a new company engaged in a dangerous enterprise. He was calling less for followers to believe a specific set of doctrines and practices and much more to a commitment to him and consequent involvement in his world-changing cause. At stake then and now is not so much particular worship ceremonies or creedal wordings as the embracing of a living reality that gives meaning to life and mission. Beyond believing, the church is to become disciples gathered together in preparation for action.

While all church members should be baptized, that doesn't mean merely submitting to a particular practice in church, with debate about how much water must be involved and how old you should be or how long you have been there or how much you know about church theology. The primary meaning of Christian baptism must be an expressing of willingness to be immersed in the love of Christ and thereby brought to newness of life in the Spirit and membership in the Spirit's fellowship on mission.

Baptism must not be merely a physical extension of the Jewish circumcision mentality sharply criticized in the New Testament. It said that you can't be a real member unless you have been cut in the approved manner. It instead must be an accepting of the commission of the church to help change the world by representing the kingdom of God now coming near in each new believer.

Pilate heard Jesus say, "For this I was born, and for this I have come into the world, to bear witness to the *truth*" (Jn 18:37). Christ's vocation is our vocation now as his people, the church. We are to be witnesses to the world about Jesus who is the truth that's intended to change everything.

People today tend to ignore mere religious speculation but may listen to a witness to actual experience of life change. Christian theology which stresses the trustworthiness and importance of life-changing religious experience is more likely to return to general favor in our postmodern setting. The best method of evangelism is personal testimony. The best way to reach another life is by being able and willing to say, "Whereas I was blind, *now I see*."

Here's a big thought to be considered seriously again. The church of Jesus is to be concerned less with its own preservation and more with being a light willing to be expended as necessary by its penetration of the world's darkness. The life of the church is saved only by being lost in self-sacrificing mission. To be lost this way is to be found!

The yeast of the church exists not to be maintained but to be consumed in the dough, making it rise to become more edible. By contrast, the church as institution will tend to go to extraordinary lengths to preserve itself and become less and less relevant to others. It's time to think seriously about how to avoid preservation at the expense of mission!

The Order of the Yoke

Here is strong language no longer to be ignored. "Christ came not to propose mild religious innovation but to cast fire on the earth. Inadequate kindling as we are, we disciples of Jesus nevertheless are called to be the components of a Christ conflagration."[86] Rather than forming new denominations and polishing old practices, it's time to embrace the post-denominational age, with each congregation actively identifying with the *whole church* as opposed to highlighting only some separated segment of it. It's human to tribalize; it's divine to universalize.

It was David Elton Trueblood who once dreamed of the "order of the yoke." Such a grouping of believers would not try to supplant existing church structures but work for renewal within and beyond them. His vision was of a fresh "monasticism" that features serious discipline and sacrifice without the traditional walls that separate believers from each other and the world. Elton had been inspired by his visit to the Iona fellowship in Scotland and its rhythm of withdrawal and encounter considered basic to the Christian vocation.[87]

The critical conclusion was this. "One of the most encouraging ideas which has entered my mind is that we again are *early Christians* still alive while the faith is fluid and capable of assuming new forms." An ideal image of the Christian community is "the order of the yoke." Believers choose to be bound together in self-sacrificing service for the Master.

A similar vision is seen in the recent creation of the Wesleyan Holiness Connection now working for renewal within a network of more than a dozen denominations and their numerous programs and institutions. The WHC is not an "organization" so much as the banding together in fellowship for more effective mission. Leaders gather for inspiration and scatter for increased impact. Whatever the renewal thrust of today's church, it should carry the dynamic of what is reported in Matthew 11:25-30.

The act of "take my yoke upon you" is what's required if the vitality of the Christian faith is to be recovered. Being bound to Christ means accepting a discipline that leads paradoxically to a new kind of freedom. It spawns a fellowship because yokes are not to be worn alone. To be the church, Christians are to be in active community, yoked with others because they have chosen to be yoked with Christ. When commonly yoked, impact in the world is maximized.[88]

It's time to think and deeply about this. "The church serves the gospel of Christ and a lost world best when it derives its life and legitimacy, its vision and standards, from *the Christian gospel*. The pivotal task of the church is to be people who really live in light of

God's reign and by the Spirit's grace and power in the *now* of Christ mission in the world."[89]

The church of Jesus should be understood by an unusual use of the verb *to be*. The church is that body of believers in Jesus Christ dedicated to being God's people advancing the *is-ness* of the *shall be* of God's reign. The church lives on behalf of that for which it yet waits. Its people live in the tension between the age to come and this present evil age. The constant challenge is to actually *be* the church, aware of its special identity and determined to be that which it is called to be, lovingly *in*, *for*, and *over against* "the world."

Should We Abolish the Laity?

The demands of church leadership are great indeed. Pastors today are God's specially anointed and need as much preparation and ongoing support as possible. Credentialing divinely called leaders is appropriate religiously and often necessary legally. Even so, we need to think again about the meaning of being a Christian "minister." If the average church would take seriously the notion that every lay member is really a minister of Christ, we could have a religious revolution in a relatively short time.

Millions of believers are merely backseat Christians, very willing to be observers of the performances which religious professionals stage, ready to criticize or applaud, but hesitant to consider the possibility of active front-line participation themselves. Here lies a fundamental weakness of the contemporary church. All members of the church are to be key players in church mission, not spectators in the stands.

Who is a Christian minister? How many ministers are in your church? Are they called "Lead," "Executive," "Associate," or what? Who then are the laypersons? Presumably they are everyone else, the religiously "unemployed" comprising the bulk of the fellowship laying about. If this is the case, *we must think again!*

Tony Campolo titled his writing about David Elton Trueblood "*The Quiet Revolutionary*," explaining this way. "For over 50 years Elton Trueblood has carried on a crusade to *abolish the laity*."[90] This meant at least doing away with rigid distinctions between laity and clergy. The first talk about this appeared in his *The Essence of Spiri-*

tual Religion (1936) based on sermons he had delivered as Acting Dean of the chapel at Harvard University. The central point was that Christianity withers when it's a spectator sport played by a few and watched by the many.

A layman in medicine is one who cannot practice being a doctor. The same is true in law, but it must be very different in the church. There must be no place in the Christian fellowship for those who cannot or will not *practice the faith*. There are to be no paying and sleeping passengers on the ship of Christ. We are not on vacation, cruising at our leisure, leaving all the work to the professional crew.

There's no chance of victory in a military campaign if ninety percent of the soldiers are untrained and uninvolved. Early Christians sought God's will in a fellowship far more intense than sitting together in a room listening to a religious homily. They may have begun in an Upper Room at first, but soon they had left to hit the many streets of the world with good news.

Early Christians were not an audience. They were actors in the bright lights on stage. They were members of a "company of the committed." They were not to think of the church's "sacraments" as mandatory religious practices to be followed precisely to avoid their Christianity being questioned. Instead, they were to embrace a much larger vision of "sacrament," understood as God seeking to be Self-revealed through the material aspects of this physical world, actions full of meaning, nature full of beauty, events evidencing divine action, people shining with Spirit life.[91]

All believers should be taught that they are called, gifted, and in baptism "ordained" to the Christian ministry. Ministry is much broader than what we commonly call credentialed leadership.[92] This bigger vision avoids any believer retreating from "the world" in order to avoid its evil or sitting on a pew gladly observing someone else's service for Christ. There is a yoke for all. Ministry is inspired by faith rising from the depths of a living encounter with the God.

All believers should know an unworldly worldliness inspiring them to encounter the world and anxious be *in it* while consciously not *of it*. Such unworldly believers in the world have become ministers active in the fields of education, politics, scholarship, etc., deliberate agents of Jesus wherever they are. True godliness doesn't "turn men and women out of the world, but enables them to live better in it, and excites their endeavors to mend it."[93]

The call to Christian "mending" always should heed the caution stated above by John Howard Yoder. Christian presence in the world is not to be one of a desired sovereignty, hoping to soon rule the world with Christian beliefs, but one of servanthood whereby believers lay down their lives on the world's behalf.

When in the world a servant way, the constant attitude becomes reverence for the divine wherever found. It's also the parallel role of being tough-minded, prepared to encounter and engage the skeptic, the hypocrite, the confused and lost. This has been called "rational evangelicalism." Whatever the name, it's a type of Christian existence so needed today. Spiritual experience with Christ is essential. So then is an active mind that cautions about the frequent downsides of spiritual experience and the accommodations of Christian congregations and whole denominations. This can only be done well when yoked together as the true church on mission.

The result of rational evangelicalism is "a revered Bible, but without idolatry; a loved humanity, but without sentimentality; an upholding of divine sovereignty, but without denial of human freedom; and a realization that each person is inclined to sin and yet never forsaken by the heavenly visitant."[94] All this drives a believer into the fellowship of Jesus and then together and lovingly out into the world.

If Christians are to live out their callings as ministers, they need the help that comes through small-group experiences within the larger life of the church. Christians need to function as priests to each another, a mutual building up for ministry, each finding spiritual renewal and guidance for living out the calling of service in the world.

If you are a Christian, you *are a minister*. The laity should be abolished when it's thought of as the unemployed and uncircumcised believers. Baptism is a commissioning to the demanding service of ministry employment. It's a yoking for every true believer.

Thoughtful believers should be concerned with the future because that's the only area of human experience about which anything can be done. We cannot change the past, and the present is gone as soon as reported. The future, however, is the coming reality about which we still can make a difference. Doing so will take us all, all yoked together as the faithful ministering church.

Remember the encounter of Jesus with a lawyer who wanted to know exactly who Jesus meant by "the neighbor." Should our neighbor be understood only as a person of Jewish descent whose legal residence is within a radius of less than three kilometers from our own? The answer of Jesus was the story of a Good Samaritan. It makes the point that a neighbor is *anyone who needs help*. Who then is a Christian minister? Every agent of Jesus traveling the troubled roads of the world in search of those lost and in trouble. Think seriously about this again!

Chapter Eleven

Christ-Centered Christian Universities

> If a university does not remain Christ-centered, eventually it will dissipate in its commitments and distinctives. It will drift into an eventual secularism. However, if it remains Christ-centered, it can provide the world with a vibrant mission, a powerful Christian worldview through the eyes of Christ, and robust Christian values to live by. –Jonathan S. Raymond, *Higher Higher Education*

> There is a crying need for Christian intellectuals. The Christian, if to be effective in our confused world, must love God *with all the mind*. – David Elton Trueblood, *While It Is Day*

We have insisted that it's crucial to think again about many things related to Christian faith. Included have been the importance of spiritual experience, real encounters with God and not just thinking and theorizing about these things. The world urgently needs witnesses about the way to a better tomorrow.

If these witnesses fail to appear thoughtful and aren't well prepared to live credible spiritual lives emerging from their thinking, they will not be heard. It was Charles Wesley who said wisely, "Unite the pair so long disjoined, knowledge and vital piety." His brother John worked hard at the task of clarifying Christian knowledge while he put it into beautiful verse that the churches could sing with all their hearts.

Therefore, within today's Christian community there needs to be quality discipleship preparation, education, systematic help for believers to learn to think and speak convincingly about the faith and its redemptive relations to today's culture. Programs for mentoring disciples in the churches are vitally important. So is addressing new generations needing to make a living and hoping while doing so make a difference for Jesus in all walks of life.

Jesus is the One who gives life itself. For this to become thoughtfully clear and its cultural relevance enabled for new generations, consideration now must be given to the existence of quality and clearly Christian universities.

Can an institution of higher education be "Christian"? At least in origin and stated mission, many currently are. The problem is that in actual function many of these hardly are anymore. To avoid loss of actual identity, constant intentionality is required. We have said that there is one stable place to stand as Christians, the Person and truth of Jesus Christ himself. Accordingly, a Christian university must intentionally remain truly *Christ-centered* throughout the several dimensions of its ongoing life. Institutional inertia often is headed the other way.

Our human behavior reflects who we are in the center of our very beings. A Christian university, necessarily a human institution, must first reflect outwardly what it's supposed to be at its very center. What is that? It's to be a real community of Christian faith particularly dedicated to quality learning processes *in light of Jesus Christ*. While not the church, such a university nonetheless must consciously serve the church's mission by instructing students in careful thinking designed to know the faith and develop effective ways to represent it cogently to a skeptical world.

Christians gathered for mission work within any endeavor, business, education, medicine, engineering, etc., should focus on being an alert and well-informed *faith community.* In the setting of an educational campus, the institutional gatherings necessarily serve various purposes standard to higher education. If, however, the initial and essential focus of faith-community-on mission is neglected, the mechanics of organized life soon will tend to overwhelm all else.

Institutions are prone to perpetuate themselves, even at the expense of their distinctive missions. Being constantly intentional about first being a *Christian* community is essential or the university will fail in this vital purpose. If relegated to a secondary additive, likely over time it will devolve into rote religious activities without transformational power. This is how Christian schools lose their path and abdicate their Christian influence.

Much like people, when an institution defines itself more in terms of what it *does* than what it *is*, that institution will fall prey to becoming mostly the servant of institutional inevitabilities. In the race to outperform, keep up, expand, stay competitive, be respected, the church school can lose its soul and become the victim of strong "outside" forces.

It has happened so often. Deep Christian identity is replaced with a maze of circumstantial matters. The "higher" dimension is lost in the lower preoccupations. The average Christian university is threatened with being stretched to its limits by mounting activities on the margins of its central being. Its distinctive Christian foundation is in danger of faltering.[95] We must think again about this great danger to Christian mission and how best to counter it.

The "Higher" in Higher Education

The church needs to rethink its approach to the Christian academic communities it founds and sponsors. When they are demoted to being primarily dispensers of courses and experiences designed for getting good jobs and being exciting settings for entering "adulthood," the salt will lose its saver.[96]

When student preferences and growing technology pushes their basic functions to online electronics, the power of community dissipates. When the primary reality becomes dollars, how many the education costs and how many graduation will ensure, public and private schools seem to flow into one common secular reality. What happens to the Christ core?

Of course, all schools of higher education seek to graduate persons who have matured into responsible adults with competence in their chosen fields of specialization. Christian universities, however, set the bar higher. Their intention is to produce graduates of both competence and *character*, especially Christian character on redemptive mission in today's world. "Character formation is the value-added nature of Christian higher education."[97]

The extensive coaching work of Dr. Kevin Mannoia with Christian institutions of higher education is based on this premise:

As much as parents may hope their child will "get a good job" because of the investment they've made in a college education, it is much more important that their child discover the fullness of God's call and the nature of their own identity as people who bear the image of God. In this respect, the Christian university has a dual motivation for keeping its identity well-balanced and well-formed.[98]

Precisely, but maintaining this dual motivation is no easy task. Seminaries and universities sponsored by churches are compelled to fulfill their mission to educate persons in accordance with the expectations of the academy as well as the mission of the church. Both are necessary. Christians need to be educated in this delicate mixture of goals and standards in institutions that are consciously seeking to be *Christian* faith communities.

The higher bar of these schools is implemented in various ways. Here are four common areas of confusion, pitfalls, ways often relied on in the hope that they are enough to meet the special Christian-formation aspect of church-related schools. These common areas and related pitfalls are summarized helpfully by Arthur Holmes in his classic *The Idea of a Christian College.*

Pitfall #1 is seeing the Christian college or university as fundamentally a "defender of the faith," as a place where students go to be indoctrinated in Christian faith and protected from false secular ideas. There is a serious problem with this approach. If students are simply indoctrinated with the proper responses to current non-Christian ideas, they will be unable to evaluate and interact with new ideas they will encounter over their lifetimes. A student needs a disciplined understanding of the faith's heritage plus creativity, logical rigor, and self-critical honesty, more than prepackaged sets of questions and answers about controversial current issues.

Pitfall #2 is seeing the Christian university as a place where one can get a good "secular" education with a few needed Christian add-ons (biblical studies classes, Christian activities, required chapel, etc.). This approach can't be the essence of the Christian university, according to Holmes, because one can accomplish these add-ons at a secular university through campus ministries and other resources nearby the university.

Pitfall #3 is seeing the Christian university as fundamentally aimed at full-time Christian ministry training. Holmes points to the inadequacy of this approach by distinguishing between *training* and *education*. Training develops skills and techniques for handling given materials and facts and situations. Education will include training but go beyond to include the ability to evaluate new ideas and learn new skills and techniques. The Christian campus must be engaged primarily in the task of *education*, with "ministry" understood as far more than ordained church clergy.

Pitfall #4 is seeing a Christian university as fundamentally a place where Christian students can get social and extracurricular benefits, such as finding Christian friends and possibly a Christian spouse and enjoying the advantages that come from a smaller school (more access to professors, etc.). Simply put, these things can be achieved without going to a Christian university. They aren't the fundamental purpose of a *Christian* university.[99]

All Truth Is God's Truth

The grand goal of a Christian university is to implement a core belief for the good of its students in their private lives and future vocations. All truth is *God's truth*, and a Christian university is determined to bring together the truths found in the various academic disciplines with the orienting truths revealed in Christian Scripture and God's many-faceted present work in the world.

These truths are never opposites or contradictions. What is needed on campus is the deliberate formation of cadres of capable minds ready to accept the challenges of these worlds of truth and their present relationships to each other and the surrounding culture where graduates will work and live. This is a demanding but essential task.

The hope lies in the emergence of Christian intellectuals able to meet this challenge. It's that of competence in a particular field of inquiry combined with a firm grounding in Christian truth that surrounds and informs that competence and seeks to direct its uses for human good. There is a golden biblical text for Christian intellectuals. "Always be prepared to make a defense to anyone who calls you to account for the hope that is in you, and do it with gentleness and reverence" (1 Pet 3:15).

Examining with clear Christian thought all prevailing truth claims is a skill needed by each new generation. The writings of C. S. Lewis in particular show the way around all "unexamined liberalisms." The Christian campus should be a place that develops young thinkers who are prepared to address the thought leaders of the day in needed self-examination, and be thought leaders themselves on behalf of Jesus Christ. If that's not what Christian universities currently are, they need to think again!

The combination of the love of God and the love of learning commended itself to the early colonists of America. It seemed to them eminently reasonable and essential to quality living and productive societies. Then came a pattern of disassociating knowledge and piety. Recall Thoreau's response to Emerson after Emerson had remarked that Harvard College then taught all branches of learning. "Yes, all the branches but none of the roots." Much hard new thinking needs to be done here. Christian higher education considers carefully both roots and fruits.

Three options offer themselves to colleges and universities born in the bosom of Christian faith, schools key to the cultural heritage of America. One is to let them yield to the inertia to go secular, increasingly separated from their religious roots. Another is to turn them into schools only for the training of Christian workers, particularly clergy. The superior option is to maintain them as distinctive places for seeking to demonstrate excellence in the sciences and all major studies, striving to influence positively the course of contemporary civilization, not in separation from religious roots but in close connection with them.

All searchers after truth want to do it well. The committed Christian has an added motive driving the intellectual task. It's viewed as a sacred task because it's God's truth being sought. Dishonesty in research and reporting is worse for the Christian. More than bad science, it's also blasphemy. Sloppy research and all dishonesty become sins and not merely bad form.

The claim that scholars can be wholly impartial or neutral in anything is an outmoded idea unacceptable to postmoderns. The very rejection of value judgments is itself a value judgment. To be nonreligious is to choose by faith that negative "religious" option. We all are formed by some community of faith. The Christian university believes that Jesus Christ is the superior community of truth deserving of informing all others.

The committed Christian university has and intentionally maintains a pervasive perspective. It's stated often and openly and always being examined and engaged. It's the serious search for the knowledge of God and God's universe and God's demands on human life. All of this is informed by the conviction that "humans and the world of nature are best understood as creatures of the Divine Mind who is accurately revealed in Jesus Christ."[100]

What such Christian institutions hope to produce is not merely students with wide knowledge of facts. Raw facts will shift and multiply and often are illusory. Critical is the ability to judge among presumed facts in any field of life's endeavor. Especially pursued on a Christian campus is the goal of accurate judgment of movements and faiths. Graduates are intended to be persons with inspired imaginations concerning the ways in which people of differing perspectives can live together in peace and also prepare to live in a world beyond this one. Such a grand task is so important in today's diverse and confused world.

Primary Theological Emphases

I've been privileged personally to graduate from a Christian campus strongly committed to this ideal perspective of a Christian university (Geneva College). I've been honored to serve my whole career in another such institution that moved in the 1920s from first being a Bible training school to the broader liberal arts school model (Anderson University). My doctoral dissertation at Indiana University demonstrated clearly that meaningful faculty academic freedom can function well is such distinctively Christian environments.

Wisdom is found in a presentation Richard T. Hughes delivered to the faculty of Anderson University in 2004. His lead question was, "What Makes Church-Related Higher Education 'Christian'?" His answer began with a call for such institutions to orient themselves theologically. They should seek to become authentically Christian by embracing the heart of two Christian traditions. He referred specifically to the Lutheran and Anabaptist traditions, quickly noting that it's not so much these two historically as it is what they continue to represent under various names.

They each, Hughes told the faculty, are profoundly "radical," one with a strong theology of *justification* and the other of *sanctification*. These are "two sides of the same Christian gospel." Together they provide "the strongest possible foundation for a church-related college or university to live out its Christian commitments in a consistent and holistic way." Incidentally, these two sides are quite compatible with the current postmodern mind.

First, **justification**. Church-related higher education is most deeply Christian when it reflects "a radical commitment to diversity, pluralism, and genuine academic freedom, and grounds this commitment in a Christian vision of reality." Christians believe that God alone is God. Humans are fallen, finite, and subject to many limitations, including flawed understanding.

Our justification before God is solely by *grace through faith*. Who are we to insist that we have a corner on truth that's automatically superior in all understandings of other cultures, times, and faith communities? Like the Genesis story of Jacob's night of wrestling with God, we must go on with a limp, knowing and not knowing, rooted in the reality of God without ever gaining any full comprehension about that reality.

Then, **sanctification**, the other side of the Christian truth paradox. Once set right before God, we believers must go on to activate that rightness within our total being and in relation to our total surroundings. Sanctification is the move from cross-centered forgiveness to cross-centered living, a surrender of mind and body to the ongoing mission of Jesus. Martin Luther King, Jr., insisted that radical Christianity does not conform to the values of culture but to the mandates of the gospel in judgment of culture. Faith is a *verb*, justification in action directed by the faith.

There always will be some tension between a sponsoring church and a faithful Christian institution of higher education. The local congregation tends to focus on gaining and nurturing faith in Christ, while the college or university must do more, even more that sometimes seems like the opposite of the church.

It must seek to prepare the young for real life in the world, vocational life and Christian missional life. It will seek to build on the faith assumption by pressing on students the hard faith questions of the world and the difficult demands of Christian vocation. It will clarify the need for humility about and also confidence in the faith. It will insist that the Christian calling involves self-sacrificing activation of the faith in the realities of the world as it is.

The Christian university must underline that salvation is by faith alone, thus humility, and make plain that there is to be openness to increasing diversity, thus more humility, while also sharpening the mind to think through the issues of life in the special light of the presumed ultimate reality of God in Jesus Christ.

All of these are critical and interrelated tasks, sometimes seeming almost in conflict with each other. Christian higher education, if true to itself, is no easy business with guaranteed positive outcomes. The alternative, however, is to default on a clear divine calling.

Yesterday and Tomorrow

The combination of the love of God and the love of learning commended itself to the early colonists of America. It seemed eminently reasonable, historically responsible, and needful for the future of new society. They were right. The Christian university should be a community of teachers and students who confess Jesus Christ as Savior and Lord and also are engaged responsibly in a serious search for the knowledge of God, the universe, and the divine demands on human life.

The basic Christian perspective ought to be reflected in all aspects of campus life. It's the faith conviction that both humans and the world of nature are best understood as creatures of the Divine Mind who is accurately revealed in Jesus Christ.

Students must strive to grasp this mind and become prepare to reflect it their personal and professional lives ahead. Especially hoped for is the emergence of Christian character and commitment, graduates with inspired imaginations about the best ways in which a diversity of persons can live together in peace and find the fulfillment God intends.

Chapter Twelve

One Among Many?

The exclusiveness of the Christian revelation of God lies here. No one can have an adequate view of the heart and purposes of the God of the universe who does not understand that he permitted his Son to die on the cross to reach out to all people, even people who hated him. That is who God is. –Dallas Willard

The church is not people streaming to a shrine or just making up an audience for a speaker. It's laborers of Jesus engaged together in the harvesting task of reaching the perplexed and seeking them with something so vital that, if received, will change their lives.
–David Elton Trueblood

The Christian community and its institutions face a difficult task today. This is especially because the current postmodern mentality isn't particularly concerned to prove that some people are right and others wrong. The general view is that religious perspectives are ultimately a matter of social context and personal preference. "What is right for us might not be right for you, and what is wrong in our context might in your context be acceptable or even preferable."[101]

Today's world is one of extensive diversity. It tends to place Jesus in a melting pot of the world's religions, one of several bright lights of truth available for humans to follow as each sees fit. The claim of Jesus, however, is that he is *the truth*, not *a* but *the*. This absolute claim, Jesus as *the* Word from God, must be held with humility today—and yet proclaimed confidently if actually believed.

The public tends to think the exclusive claim of Jesus is too tribal, arrogant, out of step with common wisdom. Truth is where you find it. Respect for others is an essential aspect of public civility. We Christians must readily admit at least that our Christian organizations and systems of theology clearly are not themselves part of the

Jesus' absolute truth claim. Only Jesus personally is. He's said to be the one absolute place to stand, although not necessarily our thinking about him and our organizations designed to represent him.

People well formed into the image of Christ should not be closed to the possibility of God being found in the least likely of places and by anyone. If God in Jesus Christ is the source and Lord of all, then surely the God who loves all people may be found almost anywhere that one is sincerely looking for God. After all, God is the very One in the process of looking for us all!

The "prevenience" of God means that "Christians welcome new thought and people into the circle of knowing because in that openness and acceptance they are better able to explore and find dimensions of the infinite God who has made himself known in all of creation."[102] Put otherwise, we can know and believe only because first God comes to us and gifts us with the needed knowing and believing capability. Given God's great and universal love, we should expect it to be reaching everywhere for everyone.

Presumably, given who God is known to be in Christ, such prior gifting of receptive capability isn't denied to anyone regardless of their knowledge of Christianity or the biblical revelation. We all are given freedom to choose and with it the ability to choose for or against God having come in Christ for our salvation. Christian missionaries go to bring enrichment and encouragement and resources to the world's disadvantaged. They do not go to bring God to their destinations. Wherever they go, God already is there!

Wherever Christian believers gather, there is the church. Christ is the Head of his one church and all true believers are joint members with each other of this one body (1 Cor 12). The structural dividedness now existing among believers is an unfortunate negative. Emphasizing the lines of dividedness is a churchly disease.

John Wesley saw the true church as it should be seen, the fellowship of all who, regardless of affiliation, share living faith in the one God and one Lord Jesus by means of the one Spirit of Jesus (Eph 4:4–6). He collaborated with Calvinists in evangelism, commended Catholic saints as models of sanctity, and scheduled Methodist meetings to avoid conflict with Anglican church services. Such unity of vision enables effective church mission.

The Church *Is* Mission

It's time to think again about the nature, unity, and mission of the church, the body of Christ. The church by definition is *other-oriented*. It's not instituted by God solely or at least not primarily for the personal benefit of its current members. Christ enlists ordinary men and women into his fellowship for more than "saving" them. They are saved and then commissioned to join in the saving work God.

The church should not be thought of as essential to the Christian believer merely because it brings personal inspiration and spiritual advancement. It's essential to believers because it's essential to church outsiders. It's God's instrument for the redemption of the whole world. All members have their roles in this grand engagement. To opt out of serious engagement is to undercut the very lifeblood of the church. Spiritual narcissism is a serious condition for self-centered individuals and ingrown churches.

The church must believe that the saving work of Jesus Christ was an historical event with universal significance for all times. God reaches out lovingly to every human to reclaim and restore. One aspect of John Calvin's influential thought is troubling. He taught that God withholds his saving presence and power from select persons, in fact from a majority of sinful persons. Historically, a large percentage of humanity has lived and died knowing nothing about Jesus of Nazareth. Those who have heard aren't always among "the elect."

Calvin concluded that God, *by his own choice*, will not save most sinners. All are undeserving. Some are selected by grace for salvation. Robert Barclay understandably called this assumption of divine exclusion a "blasphemous doctrine." It reduces God to being quite unlike the Son, Jesus. John Wesley and John Calvin agreed on most theological things, but not on this teaching of selective election. The whole world was Wesley's parish because he understood that all of it is God's chosen saving arena.[103]

More acceptable Christian thought is this. Given the debilitating effects of the fall into sin, no human can be saved apart from Christ. However, any spatial or temporal or number limitations on the saving work of Christ must be rejected. The only limitation is human choice against God's redeeming love. All persons need redemption and the good news is that all persons may have it if they choose. The work of Christ is universal and continuous through the present and universal work of the divine Spirit of Jesus. Jesus is "the true light who lights *every person* who comes into the world" (Jn 1:9).

Jesus seeks and can save any of us who is lost in sin, bringing the redeemed into the one church, his present body. This church must not be thought of as primarily a religious institution. It's that in part, although so much more. It includes a cloud of witnesses now departed and a host of others with no awareness of institutions with Christian labels. Some who never have touched a Bible nonetheless have been granted access to the Word that always is streaming lovingly from the Father through the Spirit. When touched and gratefully responding in faith, a person belongs.

Devoid of evangelistic mission, it's possible to have successful religious institutions called "Christian" that provide valuable services to their members and neighbors. The problem is that such limited outreach activity is hardly the church on mission as intended by Jesus. The idea of mission, far from marginal to the Christian faith, is what brings the entire Christian cause into focus. The church by its nature *is mission.*

Church members are new creations in Christ. They are to become committed disciples who choose covenant with each other, forming communities of the Spirit. Such communities stand apart from the world in order to nurture their distinctive Christ-identity. That identity involves being sent by the Spirit as saving agents to all the world.

Recall these classic words of Emil Brunner: "The church exists by mission as fire exists by burning." Fire ceases to be anything but ashes after the burning stops. Likewise, when the church becomes satisfied to hug its treasures to itself, it no longer is on fire and thus is not the church. The church to be itself must be missionally ignited by the Spirit, being an incendiary fellowship. "Jesus lit a fire and Paul used it to forge for him a church."[104]

The church of Jesus does not *have* missions; its very life *is* mission. Jesus spoke of the church as salt, light, and leaven. These represent *penetration.* Salt exists to penetrate meat, light the darkness, and leaven the dough. Why? So that each may be preserved, enlightened, and transformed. All are frustrated in their intended functions when not employed.[105]

In other words, the church exists to give itself away. What then is the purpose of a local Christian congregation? It's primarily to equip its people for mission. Congregational programs are to be evaluated in terms of their relevance to the task of preparing the people for *going*, not merely staying.

The period 1800 to 1910 was a time of great worldwide expansion of Christianity. Most Christians excitedly affirmed the validity and priority of church mission. That circumstance has changed considerably and now must be addressed. Believers must think again, and seriously. What's at stake is more than financial support for denominational mission boards. The entire Christian cause is at risk apart from focusing on the priority of its mission.

The Clear Message Is Yet Mystery

The very name of God was so sacred in Jewish tradition that care had to be taken when daring to speak it aloud or even touch it once written. One of the Ten Commandments focuses on not taking the divine name "in vain." This means more than blasphemy through verbal vulgarity. It includes representing God's name in an unworthy manner. "God" has been known by many names across cultures and centuries and religious traditions. Some, likely most, of these names have suggested something that God *is not*, or at least they have affirmed less than all that God really is. That's subtly an in-vain breaking the commandment.

Picture in your mind Christian theologian Paul Tillich sitting on a shoreline staring out at the ocean. Tears are streaming down his cheeks. He deliberately chose to avoid using the word "God" in his theological books because to him God is hardly another being alongside all other beings. He preferred to use "Ground of Being," God as the originator and base of all beings and all things.

Gazing at the ocean, picture Tillich as overwhelmed by the unimaginable immensity and inexpressible mystery. Even so, he realizes that it's a vastness as close as the sea breeze in his nostrils and the gentle wash of the wave touching his toes. That little wave is part of the whole and in its gentleness it's filled with the power of a revealing and relating love. Tillich couldn't begin to grasp it all, but it all was somehow touching and changing him.

God is not left without Self-witness in our human history. The waves of divine presence touch every shore, however much the larger mystery remains. The unknowable wishes to be known and have life-changing relationships with us struggling human beings. This amazing divine Self-revealing once came to have a name, Jesus. The paradoxical fact is that Jesus might be known, at least to a degree, even when his name never has been heard.

This universal knowing is the sacred and universal ministry of the Spirit of Jesus spreading the potential of salvation to all, whatever their time, place, or culture. Luke wrote his Gospel and its extension, the Book of Acts, to present a beautiful portrayal of the boundary-breaking early Christian faith. It was moving across human frontiers in the power of God's Spirit. Christian faith still must be in motion, still on mission.

There appear in the New Testament the classic stories of the Prodigal Son and the Good Samaritan. Jesus is shown reaching to the black sheep of society, including women, lepers, and the poor. He focuses on prayer and meditation to sustain himself against strong opposition. In spite of the negatives constantly faced, there's joy found everywhere in Luke's account. The good news of Jesus is for all, in all times, and always creating joy.

The Spirit of God still is working on behalf of salvation wherever people are opening themselves to that possibility. When they do, they are feeling the heartbeat of the Father through the ministry and graces of the Spirit, even if with no direct awareness of the historic Son. They are seeking holiness of heart and life as they can understand and implement it. The Father smiles at this and the Spirit assists it.

The loving Spirit of God is present and honoring the holiness quest of all who are reaching in faith toward the God they barely know. Even though a basic knowledge of God is universally available in this way, apart from the historic expression of God's saving activity in Jesus Christ, it's partial knowledge at best. The cross that once appeared outside Jerusalem existed in the heart of God before it ever was planted in the hard earth by crucifying Romans. The more one has opportunity to learn of this the more likely and richer will be the experience of salvation. Such is the motivation for Christian mission.

The amazing love of God is the creative and restorative force that has permeated the whole creation in all times. It was the dynamic behind Israel's Exodus from Egypt and return from Babylon's captivity. It was what caused the tomb of Jesus to become amazingly empty. One thing must be clear, however. All human response to God, directly in Jesus Christ or through him indirectly by the Spirit, is possible only because of the universal presence and working of God's grace come to its fullness in Jesus.[106]

The Christian claim is that saving divine grace was rooted in and best exemplified by the atoning work of Christ, although always active in the universal ministry of Christ's Spirit. Stress should be placed on the importance of human response to the universal availability of this grace. All are called to be holy and, by God's grace, can be holy if they choose. No one will be saved without Christ's atonement, but one need not be historically aware of that atonement to benefit from it.[107]

The Confusion of Empires

Are Christians to accept with resignation that we are living in a "post-Christian" age. Inclusion is the rule of the day. Live and let live. Accept and don't judge or try to change minds and cultures about religious and ethical matters. Colonization is a tragedy that should stay in the past. A culture should be free to develop its own lifestyle without alien pressure from any self-centered competitor.

If people want to engage in polygamy, so our day tends to think, that's their business and not that of some who prefer monogamy and claim that a revelation from above has declared what's best. Absolute tolerance should prevail. Believing in God or not is merely an available option. Christians should employ the logic of gracious non-interference. That's the current doctrine of cultural relativism.

Human cultures can be different in significant ways, despite the leveling influence of the worldwide internet. Is there no objective standard for judging one better than another, no objective reference point in the realm of moral values? Christian missionaries are said to go wrong when insisting that "foreign" people, those "living in darkness," should abandon their traditional religious beliefs and practices. Maybe those beliefs are better suited to their local situations than Christianity. So goes the thought of our day.

Is this the end of the legitimacy of Christian mission? It's time to think again! The current logic of rampant relativity must be reconsidered. It is a vulnerable dogma regardless of its popularity. Some cultures ought to change if they function in direct contrast to the values and goals of Jesus Christ that comprise the very creation plan of God. Consider the logic of the power dominance of prevailing empires.

For approximately the first three hundred years of its existence, the Christian church sought to be faithful to the teachings Jesus, seeking to be good citizens of the kingdom of God and giving to Caesar only the little that actually belongs to him. The faith spread rapidly and often was persecuted. Then came the "Constantinian Compromise."

A Roman emperor legalized the Christian faith and even made it the official religion of the Roman Empire. That encouraged the church to serve the powerful empire that elevated and protected and wanted to be used for political purposes. Such subtle shifting of primary loyalty encouraged the downfall of the church. Empires and loyalties had gotten confused and compromised. Jesus Christ was downgraded to second place.

The empire of Rome is long gone, of course, but the confusion of church loyalty remains. Many North American Christians today seem to have their first allegiance to the patriotism of their homeland rather than the divine realm that exists beyond all lands. They have lost the political meaning of Christian baptism, where Christians become part of a community that's an *alternate "empire"* transcending all racial, cultural, national, and geographic boundaries. Any human nation committed to itself is not the one to which Christians are to be ultimately loyal.

The reign of Christ is not political dominance of any piece of earthly territory, the modern nation of Israel included. Citizens of Christ, members of the church of Jesus, dare to conform to the values and goals of Christ and not to any human "fatherland." Christ's people are necessarily residents of a given land, and yet ultimately are citizens of another that transcends all human lands and patriotisms.

Human nations without exception are flawed. They are temporary constructs typically operating with values quite contrary to Christ. That includes the United States that speaks proudly of freedom for all. Such freedom on occasion can shift to selfish activity at the expense of others. The ideal is admirable while the actuality too often encourages an economy of capitalism that values acquisition and even greed, so unlike Jesus Christ. This must be thought about seriously in a time when a large portion of the Christian "evangelical" community is aligned with political forces claiming to save a "Christian" nation from the overwhelming forces of secularism.

Christian mission can go very wrong when it exports a valued home culture and political loyalty and denominational bias to other people and lands and cultures. It goes very right, however, when believers in Jesus realize that they are privileged to be part of a divine "conspiracy" to undermine the structures of evil that continue to dominate human history. The tools of this legitimate domination are "the forces of truth, freedom, and love. We are called to relentlessly align ourselves with these forces because we know what is cosmically afoot."[108]

The "Where" and "Why" of Church Mission

The nature of the Christian mission has little to do with geography. Nor is it limited to a specialized divine call for a few to go to the deepest of dark Africa or the masses of far-off India. In contrast to most religions, Christianity by nature is not local, tribal, or ethnic, but potentially available to any human being, anywhere, including the people next door. World populations are on the move today, the poor headed to the rich nations. In this fluid circumstance, it's time for Christian mission to be rethought and freshly engaged.

Admittedly, the notion of the world task of the new Christian church was limited at first by a Jewish-influenced expectation that the peoples of the world would come to Jerusalem and be instructed there (Acts 5:42). The destruction of Jerusalem in 70 A.D. helped end that assumption. The alternative would be diffusion rather than ingathering. Paul broke the shell of "parent" Judaism by insisting that the mission of the Jesus people is to "Gentiles" as well as Jews—it's for all people!

Representatives of Jesus now have gone everywhere. Sadly, there have been occasions in church history when Christian faith has been forced on other people for political reasons and even by military means. However, authentic conversions always have been those which have come by convincing minds, not forcing bodies. It's time to think again, not fight and force. The only legitimate reason for being a Christian is coming to the overpowering conviction that the Christian faith *is true*. That conviction drives one to share it boldly and yet humbly on behalf of the well-being of others.

Jesus people know that they proceed in faith. They must go in the Jesus way, knowing that truth is truth wherever found, in whatever faith community, national culture, or language construct. Any "truth" necessarily will be consistent with the truth known in Jesus Christ, for all truth is God's truth consummated in Christ.[109]

In 1938, *Time* magazine called the E. Stanley Jones "the world's greatest missionary evangelist." In India he had experienced a major reorientation of his general theological stance as a Christian missionary. At first the theology of Jones had been neatly tied up with a blue ribbon and was quite aggressive and defensive. But he came to place the securities of his Christian faith on the altar and became free to explore, appropriate any good, rejoice in truth found anywhere.

This shift of perspective allowed Jones to *love* rather than *pity* India. He now could treat all people encountered there with justice and mercy, their religious deviance from Christian beliefs notwithstanding. This was the "messy middle" that released Jones to be an "irenic force" in the world of Christian evangelism. He became Jesus to India. Because of him, thousands gladly came to Jesus.

An Indian woman once said of Jones: "Apart from the Holy Spirit, Brother Stanley would be a mess." He later reported his response: "But with the Holy Spirit I am not a mess but *a message*."[110] What a difference! Jones became a living "Yes!" to the world because God had first said a redeeming "Yes!" to him. He had become determined to find ways to express that grand positive in a non-abusive and love-laced manner.

Today's crisis in Christian mission is less financial and more intellectual. Those who believe in the mission have many tasks, but their first task is *to think!* The Bible tells us that we are to be prepared to make a defense to anyone who calls us to account for the hope that's in us (1 Pet 3:15). We go on mission not as crusaders and colonizers but because we believe deeply in something we judge very real and critically important for all people. We go to share in love and think with others when they question what we believe.

The burning motive for Christian mission is the belief that the faith is supremely *true*. It's the conviction that Christian faith conforms to reality as does no alternative known. God really is and is like Jesus Christ. Being like Christ means that God is sovereign, loving, Lord of all, including all nations, races, and cultures. Every individual has been created in the image of Jesus Christ and will benefit greatly by being restored to that image through grace and faith.

Today millions of alleged Christians are only somewhat convinced of the absolute truth of Jesus Christ. In fact, they've hardly thought about it carefully. They've come to the faith with the wrong question. "What do I personally need and think I can get out of attaching myself to this faith?" The real question should be, "Who is Jesus and what then is required of me as a follower of Christ on behalf of others?"

The effective Christian missionary is one who tells the amazing story of Jesus with all the persuasiveness possible, not with force but persuasiveness. We are called to believe, to love God with all our minds and hearts, and then go to all the world. The Christian missionary is virtually the same thing as being a Christian, for one who is not a missionary is hardly a mature Christian at all.

When we go, we are to take with us the paradox of two sayings of Jesus that seem to contradict but really don't. They rely on the word "peace," the Hebrew *shalom*. It doesn't mean the constant absence of conflict, but always the presence of fullness, wholeness, and a satisfied adequacy that survives any conflict.

Jesus said he came not to bring peace but a sword (Matt 10:34). He also left us with peace, "my peace I give to you" (Jn 14:27). He provides mission-going disciples not with the absence of struggle but surrounded with the fulfilling presence of love that enables survival in all struggle. If we have received such divine peace, we can go on mission with powerful evidence of our witness being our very lives and loving hearts.

The good news of the resurrection of Christ is supported by excellent historical evidence. The primary evidence, however, is not that the first disciples of Jesus merely believed with their minds that Jesus once rose from death. The big difference is that the risen Christ had met them personally and in his presence they had experienced dramatically changed lives themselves.

Broken and defeated men and women, the first disciples of Jesus, began to express in public a confidence that lasted for the remainder of their lives. They were immovable despite persecution and external discouragement. They were transformed people now belonging to the ever-living and ever-present Christ. They had been left with a "peace" that went beyond public understanding. They were convinced that they were proclaiming *the truth*!

One Core Commitment

The obligation of every Christian believer is to know and share belief in the transcendent and yet very present Jesus. A Jesus representative on mission has one core commitment, and it's to Christ and not to the "church" as an earthly institution. We are to share Christ, argue for Christ, model Christ, love as Christ, and spend ourselves in his mission. We are not to vigorously defend the institutionalized church, which often has elements hardly defensible. We are to proclaim the Christ who needs no defense.

It's time to think seriously about all this. The church is the Christian community where walls are broken down not by human idealism but by the work of Christ. It's the community that serves instead of rules, suffers instead of inflicting suffering, whose fellowship crosses social lines instead of reinforcing them. It's not merely the agent of a mission agency but of Jesus Christ himself.

Differing beliefs, styles of worship, and cultural backgrounds cause Christians to cluster in various ways and function separately from each other. While to a degree this seems inevitable, Christians who sanctify and orient the focus of their Christian lives around incidental differences do violence to the truth they are to represent. Primary identity must be *in Christ* and thereby among all of God's people on mission together to all the people of the world.

One of the finest fruits of the Christian revelation is the way in which it makes the church one, despite its differences. It even makes the world's religions allies rather than competitors. Anything valuable in Buddhism or Hinduism or Islam can be honored and employed because Christ has "other sheep that are not of this fold" (Jn 10:16).

Christians should never be too quick to condemn in any blanket way. The Spirit is present and work. "In many and various ways God spoke of old" (Heb 1:1). All the insights of the Hebrew prophets are enhanced by the new context which Jesus Christ provides. The same can be true of other prophets who speak from other backgrounds but are seeking to speak for the ultimate truth as best they know it.

The effect of this perspective on Christian mission is crucial. The wise Christian witness, rather than being an exponent of Western civilization or of any particular denomination, is instead the *messenger of Christ*. There is no necessity of defending the church because the missionary is not finally a servant of Christianity as an institutionalized religion. The missionary is an apostle of Jesus Christ to a far-off land or the neighbor next door.

Jesus is not an item of our culture or a tool of our church. He belongs to all cultures and is Lord of the church and the Judge of all.[111] Think again about the implications of that!

Chapter Thirteen

Think Again Before Winter Comes

Christianity is a springtime faith. Death gives way to life. Fallenness yields to risenness. The new-life resurrection of Jesus suddenly became the foundation and model of faith fulfilled *now* as well as a future promised for *then*.[112]

John Wesley said it well. "Whosoever will reign with Christ in heaven must have Christ reigning with him on earth." George Barna now adds this current concern: "We do not behave like Jesus because *we do not think like him.*"[113]

Someone said wisely that every religious question contains some element of "in spite of." We are forgiven in spite of our sins, believe by faith in spite of lack of evidence, love our neighbors in spite of their flaws and our children in spite of their behavior. We get out of bed every morning in spite of the inevitable approach of death.

There is the available alternative to the "in spite of." We should live and witness and hope *because of* Jesus, the One who has come to be with us and for us. We should do it all urgently because of the pressing need and the shortness of time.

Paul's Final Request

Paul's last letter was from a Roman prison and to a dear friend, Timothy, whom he had left in charge of the church at Ephesus. He urges Timothy to come to him in Rome. He is asked to stop at Troas on the way and pick up books and a coat that Paul had left there. It's a coat that had been "wet with the brine of the Mediterranean, whitened with the snows of Galatia, yellowed with the dust of the Ignatian

Way, and stained crimson with the blood of his wounds for the sake of Christ."[114]

Why the urgency of this request? Paul was in prison with a life sentence and likely a coming execution. It was getting cold in Rome and the need was real. "Come before winter!" (2 Tim 4:21). Come, Timothy, and bring my things please.

When winter sets in, the season for safe navigation of the Mediterranean Sea ends. If Timothy delays he will have to wait until spring, and Paul has a premonition that he may not survive that long. Speculation is that Timothy acted immediately, went to Troas, picked up the books and the old coat, sailed past Samothrace to Neapolis, then by the Ignatian Way across the plains of Philippi and through Macedonia to the Adriatic. There he took ship to Brundisium and finally up the Appian Way to Rome where he found Paul and soon would walk with him to the place of execution to see him receive a crown of glory.

Christian often brings us a "it's now or never." The days may be few for the opportunities that now lay at hand. The Christian faith offers a promised future, crowns of glory, but in the meantime calls us to function *now* on the way to being with Christ *then*. The big problem appears to be that many Christians are failing to think like Jesus, blocking their acting like him in these troubled and maybe final days. Let's think again!

Love must be central, enabling an optimism of grace. It's an expectancy that God, through the power of the Holy Spirit, can and does transform lives, renew churches, and reform societies. The key word to describe this "eschatological." It's life filled with the *love* and urgency revealed most fully in the life, death, and resurrection of Jesus Christ for the redemption of the whole world.

While all else may pass away, love never will. The crucified Jesus is risen and coming again. When the kingdom of heaven is fully established, God's love will reign supreme. But that love is intended to reign even now in human hearts and lives and communities that feature it in their worship and ministries. Wherever divine love gets expressed through acts of compassion and responses to cries for justice, there comes a transforming reality as well as a future hope.

Living and serving with a loving compassion for human wholeness and social justice is an active anticipation of heaven below.[115] Let's live like this now, being part of God's grand enterprise before winter comes! The world judges the church of Jesus by what it actually sees, not by what the church glibly announces.

Questioned should be any denominational*ism*, creedal*ism*, in fact all "*isms*" that believers use to judge each other and divide from each other, distorting their common witness to the world. Avoided should be any focus on future speculation that paralyzes the present mission of the church.

The good news is not only that Jesus is coming again but also that he already *has come* and now is working out the fruits of that victory that soon will be completed. Proper Christian faith is to be expectant about *then* in a way that makes us sense responsibility for *now*. We are to live and serve in light of the divine springtime coming after the winter that's surely near at hand.[116]

Is There Any Hurry?

The story is told of three apprentice devils coming to earth for their first assignment. They met with Satan who asked what strategy they planned. The first said, "I will tell people that there is no God."

"That will not work," said Satan, "because in their heart of hearts they know there is a God."

"Then I will tell them," said the second, "that there is no hell."

"That won't work either," replied Satan, "because there is so much evil on earth that they know there must be a hell."

The third apprentice devil said, "I will tell them there is no hurry."

"Go," said Satan, "tell them that and you will ruin them by the millions!"

When Martin Luther King, Jr., gave his "I Have a Dream" speech in 1963 on the steps of the Lincoln Memorial, he trumpeted this. "We have also come to this hallowed spot to remind America of the fierce urgency of *now*."

What a phrase that is, "the fierce urgency of now." Some things simply can't be put off. There are doors of opportunity open before us only today. If we don't take advantage of them, by springtime they may be forever shut. What is our human life? We are a mist that appears for a little while and then vanishes" (Jam 4:13-14). We are a vapor, dust in the wind, like the grass of the field that is here today and gone tomorrow.

We must act while we can. Paul needed his coat and books as quickly as possible. When will Jesus return? We don't know. We do know this.

> Time, like an ever-rolling stream,
> Bears all its sons away;
> They fly, forgotten as a dream
> Dies at the opening day.[117]

So we pray, "Teach us to number our days that we may gain a heart of wisdom" (Ps 90:12). Paul advised us to "redeem the time" (Eph 5:16), make every minute count. When it's known that death is near, the mind finally concentrates its focus. Most of the time we aren't aware of death's timing so we slide by thoughtlessly, unfocused, paying little attention. It's now time to think again!

On his retirement from Earlham College in 1966, David Elton Trueblood was named "Professor at Large." He built a home adjacent to that Indiana campus where he lived until 1988. During these years he enjoyed the role of counselor and encourager to faculty, students, and others who came to visit him at his home or in the Teague Library close by.

Professor Trueblood particularly enjoyed helping young writers with constructive criticism and encouragement—me being one. He wrote his personal autobiography, *While It Is Day*, many years before his death, anxious to record his memories and insights before the winter of forgetfulness set in. At his encouragement, I have done the same with my *A Pilgrim's Progress* (fourth ed., 2024). Timing is important. Share and serve when you still can.

Christians enjoy a springtime faith. Gorgeous little buds already are on the trees of the world despite the chill still in the air. It's surely time to think again, act decisively, particularly learn how to *think like Jesus*.

A worldview is a mental and spiritual lens through which we interpret reality. It's a filter used to put things into context and enable proper responses to them. It enables making sense of the world by organizing information in a particular way and allowing choices consistent with what we believe to be most true and significant. It's what enables us to distinguish right from wrong, good from bad, useful from useless.

For the Christian, the only acceptable worldview is the "mind of Christ" (Rom 12:2; 2 Cor 10:3-5; Col 2:8). We are called to have our minds renewed so that we can discern properly what is reality and the will of God and who is the real enemy against whom we wage. It's in Christ alone that the fullness of proper vision resides.

The Winter of Today

The extensive current research of George Barna has learned of some unfortunate reality. Today fewer than ten percent of "born-again" Christians in the United States possess a biblical worldview! This is tragic and wholly unacceptable! It undercuts church life and blocks world mission.

The Bible is an ancient book and yet one with a very modern message. The multitude of theories, facts, and techniques that have emerged in recent centuries have no clear bearing on the ultimate issues of life and destiny. They too often serve only to distract and confuse people already harassed by relentless advertising in our consumer-crazed society.

We wade about in a flood of slogans, labor-saving devices, and a blizzard of promises about when and how happiness can be achieved. Regarding our knowledge of ultimate reality and the eventual well-being of the human self, nothing has changed fundamentally since the time of Jesus.[118] What C. S. Lewis said about Narnia in *The Lion, the Witch, and the Wardrobe* is memorable and still meaningful.

The wicked witch was causing it to always be winter and never Christmas. What a hollow condition of despair. No hope. Empty suffering, much like it would be if there had been no resurrection of Jesus. Imagine the hopelessness if Calvary had been the awful and actual end of Jesus. The disciples would have dispersed in shocked despair and there never would have been a church. There would have been no good news, just another dead imposter with disgraced former disciples.

The final destination of Jesus, however, was not the cross or grave but the resurrection, the ascension, and seating on the throne of glory. He went through the cross and beyond the grave to get to our hearts with a perfect picture of the heart of the Father. Now he's asking us to go through a cross to get to our personal resurrection and become part of his ongoing mission in the world.

This is a desperate time for the world. Whether admitted or not, it's now difficult to be a real follower of Jesus Christ. Read again the preceding chapters. There is no other conclusion to draw. No matter what topic is chosen to examine, the deeper the evaluation the more certain one can be that the nations are in trouble and moving in the wrong and likely tragic direction.

Especially in the Western world, morals now are more representative of Sodom and Gomorrah than of the kingdom of God. People's religious beliefs have only a tangential and diminishing relationship to the teachings of the Bible. Trust and confidence in the institutions designed to foster appropriate living, from churches to government agencies, are plummeting. The political system has turned chaotic and unproductive, and most Americans no longer believe that the existing system, or at least those running it, is serving them well. The Christian church remains divided and isn't agreed on how to make a real difference.[119]

This sad assessment goes on. People's lifestyles are characterized by behavior and goals quite opposite those that reflect the image of God. To judge from the typical news reports, humans are largely selfish, pleasure-seeking, lust-filled, consumer-oriented, jealous, quarrelsome, greedy, dishonest, violent, and unfaithful people.

Are we listening to the wrong news source? Perhaps humankind has always fit this fallen profile. Those who diligently seek God's righteousness recognize such deficiencies and need to think again, pursuing forgiveness and restoration and a gaining of the mind and mission of Christ, and before winter comes!

Here's the question of our present time. How can the church be a healing force and not a mirror reflecting more of the problem? It's time to think seriously about all this again. The greatest challenge of today's church is not finding the right religious words or building the right structures of ministry. The real proof of the faith is in the actual *being and doing* of the Christian life. Any renewed public confidence in the truthfulness and integrity of Christian convictions will come only from the concrete *embodiment* of such convictions.

Biographer Howard A. Snyder refers to B. T. and Ellen Roberts as "populist saints." He doesn't claim that these very human persons of generations back were spiritually spotless and perfect role models for today. They did, however, seek aggressively to live lives of freedom, holiness, and justice that was for *all the people,* especially for the poor.

Why did they live that way? Because that's what B. T. and Ellen saw in Jesus Christ and they knew it was the mind he wanted them to have for their own. For this reason they are worthy examples for Christians today who are being called to engage contemporary culture with the life-transforming potential of Christian holiness. The best witness to the reasonableness of Christian faith today may not be found in well-polished rational arguments. Think humbly about that.

The best verification of our faith likely must now consist of the *changed lives* to which the church can point and for which it is responsible. In the gap between vision and reality, between the kingdom of God to come and the one very much not yet, what really counts is the choice we make *in the gap*. Winter is coming. We must think and act now, like Christ, for Christ, and for all his loved and lost children.

The heroic disciple will hear Jesus well and dare to enact what's heard. Jesus once delivered the "Sermon on the Mount" and a thoughtful believer now will realize that "it's imperatives are intended as historical possibilities. They are meant to be incarnated in our every thoughts and actions *in this life*. Whereas so many believers find ways around the 'hard sayings' of Jesus, we must actually seek to live them out."[120]

Such faithfulness is a sure sign of the soon-coming kingdom of God already to be arriving in the faithful people of Jesus. So be it!

The Present-ness of the Future

I conclude with a flurry of paradoxes that should characterize our Christian faith today and set the agenda for our present action before winter sets in and activity must cease. About these observations we must think again, seriously and soon.

The God who is biblically revealed is both *high* and *nigh*, mighty and merciful, standing eternally high above all creation while also being intimately involved in the creation's ongoing life. Christian belief is that the high of God became clearer to humans as the nigh of God when God breached the divine-human gap by coming to us lost humans *in person*. God came in Jesus Christ to identify with us, be Self-revealed to us, and be near us in an unexpectedly humble way. From so far, God lovingly came so near.

The grace of God the Father was once with us in the Son's life, death, and resurrection, and now comes to us in the "communion of the Holy Spirit." This three-part story of the one God moves from the sovereign God who becomes known through his servant Son to a continuous ministry of divine revelation and redemption through the Spirit of Jesus. The stunning fact of this divine drama is that *it has not yet ended*. This Jesus, itinerant preacher from Galilee killed at the height of a Jewish Passover celebration, has been more alive after his death than before!

The life story of Jesus the Christ is still in process, and with no end in sight. He was successfully executed and still lives eternally. The Eternal One has accepted death into his own grieving heart so that the sin of the creation can be atoned and its true life restored. The One who once died is life itself. The God-man once departed back to heaven remains with us here on earth.

We who accept this marvelous story by faith are "saved," *but not yet*. The Christian statement "I am saved" should be followed with a comma and not a period. We have yet to grow up into the full stature of Jesus Christ.

On the lips of every Christian saint have been humble words of honest confession, words like "not that I have already attained" or "the more I know the more I realize how very little I really know" or "I believe, help my persistent unbelief."

Salvation is presented in the New Testament in all tenses, past, present, and yet future. We were saved (Rom 8:24), we are being saved (1 Cor 15:2), and we shall be saved (Rom 5:9). These are all found in one verse. "Therefore, being justified by faith, we have peace with God through our Lord Jesus Christ, through whom also we have access by faith into the grace wherein we stand, and rejoice in hope of the glory of God" (Rom 5:1).

Paul was thinking grand thoughts indeed. Salvation is looking back to the time when the believer received God's forgiveness in Christ, rejoicing in the present realities of the grace wherein we stand, and looking forward in faith to the time when we shall be like Christ, when every knee shall bow and sin and death will be no more. Our salvation *was* provided, *is* being matured, and eventually *will be* fully realized.

For disciples of Jesus, there must be no disconnect between *now* and *then*. Because of what God has been doing, we now must be part of God's ongoing action. While anticipating what actions of God are yet to come, we dare not abandon the present time. We are to act courageously in the present with the resources of the future already being made available.

I once read a disturbing poem in which it is said that clocks in saloons typically are set fifteen minutes ahead of the clocks in the outside world. The reason? "This makes us a rather advanced group, doing our drinking in the unknown future, immune from the cares of the present, safely harbored one-quarter of an hour beyond the woes of the contemporary scene."[121] How escapist for the saloon patrons and how wrong for the church!

The kingdom of God both has arrived in Jesus and is not yet fully here. It is *near* and yet not altogether *here*. Christians have hope and are to live actively now from that hope. We must stop speculating about the details of God's future and start serving, living the Christ-life in the power of Christ's Spirit who already is here and bringing to us the power of the future.

How should the church, as an emissary from elsewhere, conduct itself as it lives between heaven and earth, between here and here-after? The church is to be that body of believers dedicated to being an advancing actualization of the *is-ness* of the *shall be*. Believers are to participate now in that toward which they point. This should be the day when tomorrow happens--through us by the grace of the Spirit of Jesus!

"The church should be nothing short of that fellowship of tomorrow's people who are sharing with Christ the urgent task of rearranging the realities of today's world. Then, some day, with time behind us, eternity before us, and the redeemed of all ages around us, there will be heaven, our final and forever home."[122]

Final Thoughts

It's time to think very carefully, even about the business of the value of human thinking. This is a day of great confusion. I believe that there is built into the creation a reason and rhythm that comes from beyond our merely human sphere. It's personal, grace-full, and seeking to pull us toward our destiny of life beyond all death.

We anxious humans tend to focus on the many deaths among the fragile people whom we know. We are so aware of much grief across our years. We must learn to shift focus to the life beyond death, to tomorrow's life that's present already. We must find and live out of the joy that overcomes grief and sees the hope that seeks our attention and life commitment.

This is the bigger picture that can make all the difference now as well as later. Why the excitement that surrounds all this? "For the Lord our God Almighty reigns!" (Rev 19:6). Here's the central fact known by Jesus and crucial for us to learn. Caiphas, Pilate, Herod, and Caesar of Jesus' day all soon became little more than dust beneath the chariot wheels of time. Jesus was helpless in their hands, or so they thought. Now they are mere memories of a distant yesterday while Jesus is the hope of today and the heaven that will be tomorrow. *Hallelujah!*[123]

The church should be nothing short of the fellowship of tomorrow's people sharing with Christ the urgent tasks of rearranging the realities of today's world by the power of the Spirit of all time. Someday, with time behind us, eternity before us, and the redeemed of all ages around us, there will be heaven.

In the meantime, Jesus people must refuse to be paralyzed by the idea of an eventual paradise. The church must be about God's business *now*. The church must not be merely waiting for a distant reality to arrive. It's already here, seeking to be *in us* and then *through us* for the sake of the lost world *around us*. Jesus once made this dramatic announcement.

"Times up! God's kingdom *is here*. Change your life" (Mk 1:15, *The Message*). Change to what? Change to God's intended freedom and mission. In "salvation," God sets a person free from the dominance and destiny of sin. This freedom releases life so that we are able to be the people we were created to be, people in the image of God who is love, people commissioned to bring this good news to others.

No one is ready to really live "here and now" until matters of the "there and then" are faced. The fruits of *then* are to be emerging and applied *now*. When thinking this way, Jesus believers become transformed into resident aliens, present agents of God's coming tomorrow, at work in a secular culture headed in a very different direction.

It's surely time to think with the mind of Christ and start doing something concrete about it right away! Our faith is intended to be a *lifestyle*, a special way of being in the world. That way is nonviolent, shared, loving, life by and through the ministry of the Spirit. Too often over the centuries we declared believers have made the Jesus faith into an established religion, avoiding radical life change, even being warlike, greedy, racist, selfish, and vain in the living out of the faith. "The world has no time for such silliness anymore. The suffering on Earth is too great!"[124]

Let's think again. Let's be changed ourselves by the love of Christ and then become true disciples of Jesus, God's change agents in this world!

Endnotes

1 Barry L. Callen, *Discerning the Divine*, 2004, and *Heart of the Matter*, 2016.

2 Eric Weiner, *Man Seeks God: My Flirtations with the Divine*, 2011.

3 Eric Weiner, *Man Seeks God: My Flirtations with the Divine*.

4 Title of a classic work of Christian contemplative prayer by an unknown author and dating back to the fourteenth century.

5 Stanley J. Grenz, *A Primer on Postmodernism*, 1996.

6 Compare Keith Ward, *Confessions of a Recovering Fundamentalist* (Cascade Books, 2019).

7 In *Beneath the Surface* I highlighted the consistent theological themes common to the Old and New Testaments. In *God As Loving Grace* I focused on the core characteristic of God's very being, the eternal fixed that necessarily frames all the fluids. In *The Heart of the Matter* I regularly brought discussion of all theological issues back to the person of Jesus.

8 G. K. Chesterton, in Weiner, *Man Seeks God*.

9 See David McKenna's memoir *Seeing All Things Whole*, 2024.

10 Cheryl Bridges Johns in the *Wesleyan Theological Journal*, 1999.

11 Stanley Hauerwas and William Willimon, *Resident Aliens*, 25th anniversary ed., 2014.

12 The thinking of Hauerwas and Willimon in Barry L. Callen, *Golden Nuggets of Truth*, 2024. The dramatic social change is well documented in the research work of George Barna.

13 For extended discussion of this big intellectual divide of today, see Stanely Grenz, *A Primer on Postmodernism*, 1996.

14 These two ways are highlighted in the contrasting philosophic thinking of Aleis de Tocqueville, a French political scientist, and Antonio Francesco Gramsci, an Italian Marxist philosopher. Many names could be added to each way of thinking. They are clashing, even violently, today.

15 See Barry L. Callen, *Christian Holiness*, 2023.

16 Barry L. Callen, *Bible Stories for Strong Stomachs*, 2017.

17 See books like Barry L. Callen's *Authentic Spirituality*, 2nd ed., 2006, and Kevin W. Mannoia's *Masterful Living*, 2011, and the many books by philosopher-theologian David Elton Trueblood.

18 Richard Rohr, *Yes, And. . . . : Daily Meditations*, 2013.

19 Barry L. Callen, *The Heart of the Matter*, rev. ed. 2016.

20 Brian D. Mclaren, in his Foreword to Frederick Buechner, *Secrets in the Dark: A Life of Sermons*, 2007.

21 See this trilogy developed in Barry L. Callen, *God As Loving Grace*, 1996, reprint 2018.

22 See Clark H. Pinnock, *Most Moved Mover*, 2019, and Arthur Wainwright, *Trinity in the New Testament*, 2001.

23 Dallas Willard, *The Divine Conspiracy*, 1998.

24 Elton Trueblood, in *Christianity Today*, Feb. 11, 1991.

25 Hans urs von Balthasar.

26 Thomas C. Oden, *Classic Christianity*, 2009.

27 An excellent overview is in Stanley Grenz and Roger Olson, *20th-Century Theology*, 1992.

28 Thomas Oden's autobiography, *A Change of Heart*, 2022.

29 D. Elton Trueblood, *The New Man for Our Time*, 1970.

30 See Malcolm Muggeridge, *The End of Christendom*, 1980.

31 D. Elton Trueblood, *The New Man for Our Time*, Ibid.

32 Richard J. Foster in his Foreword to Dallas Willard's *The Divine Conspiracy*, 1998.

33 See Howard A. Snyder, *The Radical Wesley*, and Barry L. Callen, *Radical Christianity*, 1999.

34 See Stanley Hauerwas and William H. Willimon, *Resident Aliens*, 25th anniversary ed., 2014.

35 Clark H. Pinnock, *Flame of Love*, 2nd ed., 2022.

36 D. Elton Trueblood, *The New Man for Our Time*, 1970.

37 Elton Trueblood, *While It Is Day*, 1974.

38 Elton Trueblood, *Philosophy of Religion*, 216.

39 In his *Philosophy of Religion*, 1957, Trueblood reviews these several features, the scientific, moral, aesthetic, historical, and religious.

40 Barry L. Callen, *Caught Between Truths*, 2007.

41 Eric Weiner, *Man Seeks God*, 2011.

42 See Marvin R. Wilson, *Our Father Abraham: Jewish Roots of Christian Faith*, 1989.

43 See Barry L. Callen, *Anchored and Reaching: The Visionary Life and Ministry of Kevin Mannoia*, 2024.

44 Alfred North Whitehead, *Science and the Modern World*, 1941.

45 Thomas C. Oden, *Classic Christianity*, 2009, and Dennis F. Kinlaw, *Lectures in Old Testament Theology*, 2010.

46 See Shirley C. Guthrie, *Christian Doctrine*, rev. ed. 1994.

47 Richard Rohr, *Yes, And. . . : Daily Meditations*, 2013.

48 Jason E. Vickers, *Minding the Good Ground*, 2011.

49 See Don Thorsen, *The Wesleyan Quadrilateral*, 2005.

50 See Don Thorsen, *Calvin and Wesley*, 2013.

51 D. Elton Trueblood, *While It Is Day*, 1974.

52 See especially Robert Barclay, *The Apology*, the standard exposition of Quaker thinking.

53 John A. Morrison, in Anderson University's *Alumni News*, 1957.

54 David Elton Trueblood thinks similarly about the arguments for God's existence. Each is plausible but not wholly convincing. Taken together, however, they form a strong web of high plausibility.

55 Howard Snyder and Joel Scandrett, *Salvation Means Creation Healed*, 2011.

56 See Chana Ullmann, *The Transformed Self*, 1989.

57 Eric Weiner, *Man Seeks God*, 2011.

58 See detail in Malcolm Muggeridge, *Jesus*, 1975.

59 This line of thought is developed in the classic book *Mere Christianity* by C. S. Lewis.

60 D. Elton Trueblood, *Robert Barclay*, 1968.

61 See Don Thorsen, *The Wesleyan Quadrilateral*, 2005, 2018, for extended discussion.

62 See Barry Callen, with Steve Hoskins, and Jonathan Powers, *A Year with Rabbi Jesus,* vol. 2, 2022.

63 William Temple, *Nature, Man and God.*

64 Verse one of D. Elton Trueblood's hymn "Baptism by Fire."

65 Randy L. Maddox, *Responsible Grace*, 1994.

66 Howard A. Snyder, *Signs of the Spirit*, 1997.

67 Richard Rohr, *Yes, And. . . : Daily Meditations*, 2013.

68 Cheryl Bridges Johns, *Re-enchanting the Text: Discovering the Bible as Sacred, Dangerous, and Mysterious*, 2023.

69 D. Elton Trueblood, *The Company of the Committed*, 1961.

70 D. Elton Trueblood, *While It Is Day*, 1974.

71 Malcolm Muggeridge, "Another King," a sermon delivered in Edinburgh, Scotland, 1968.

72 Song "Will Your Anchor Hold in the Storms of Life?" by Priscilla J. Owens.

73 Thomas Merton, *Thoughts in Solitude*, 1956.

74 Georgia E. Harkness, *Understanding the Christian Faith*, 1992.

75 Dallas Willard, *The Divine Conspiracy*, 1998.

76 Dallas Willard, op. cit.

77 C. S. Lewis, *Mere Christianity,* reprint 2023.

78 Stanley J. Grenz, *Revisioning Evangelical Theology*, 1993.

79 See Barry L. Callen's biography of Kevin W. Mannoia, *Anchored and Reaching*, 2024.

80 Kevin W. Mannoia, *Masterful Living*, 2012.

81 D. Elton Trueblood, *Robert Barclay*, 1968.

82 See Barry L. Callen, *Christian Holiness*, 2023.

83 See Barry L. Callen, *Radical Christianity,* 1999.

84 J. H. Oldham, *Life Is Commitment.*

85 Dallas Willard, *The Divine Conspiracy,* 1998.

86 D. Elton Trueblood, *The Incendiary Fellowship*, 1967.

87 D. Elton Trueblood, *While It Is Day*, 1974.

88 See Trueblood's book *The Yoke of Christ,* 1958.

89 Barry L. Callen, *Radical Christianity,* 1999.

90 Tony Campolo in the periodical *Christianity Today.*

91 See William Temple's chapter "The Sacramental Universe" in *Nature, Man, and God*, 1934.

92 Howard A. Snyder, *Liberating the Church*, 1996.

93 William Penn, *Works,* vol. 1.

94 D. Elton Trueblood, *Robert Barclay*, 1968.

95 See James Burtchaell, *The Dying of the Light*, 1998.

96 Kevin W. Mannoia has worked with many Christian institutions of higher education worldwide to urge such thinking. See especially his *Expressing Life*, 2023. A leading exponent of Christian higher education at its best is David L. McKenna, president of three such institutions. See his two-part memoir, *The Triumphs of His Grace,* 2023, and *Threads of His Grace,* 2024.

97 Jonathan S. Raymond, *Higher Higher Education*, 2015.

98 Mannoia, *Expressing Life,* 2023.

99 Arthur F. Holmes, T*he Idea of a Christian College*, 1987. A case study of the institutions of one church body that has sought to deal properly with these pitfalls is in Barry L. Callen, *Enriching Mind and Spirit*, 2007.

100 See Howard Lowry, *The Mind's Adventure*, 1950.

101 See Stanley J. Grenz, *A Primer on Postmodernism*, 1996.

102 Kevin W. Mannoia, *Masterful Living*, rev. ed., 2012.

103 See Don Thorsen, *I AM Who I AM*, 2025.

104 Frederick Buechner, *Beyond Words,* 2004.

105 David Elton Trueblood, T*he Validity of the Christian Mission*, 1972.

106 See Barry L. Callen, *God As Loving Grace*, 1996, 2018.

107 Clark H. Pinnock, *A Wideness in God's Mercy*, 1992, and John E. Sanders, in *Christian Scholar's Review,* 1994.

108 Dallas Willard, *The Divine Conspiracy*, 1998.

109 David Elton Trueblood, *The Validity of the Christian Mission*, 1972.

110 E. Stanley Jones, *Song of Ascents*, 1968.

111 David Elton Trueblood, *A Place to Stand*, 1969.

112 Barry L. Callen, *Radical Christianity*, 1999.

113 George Barna, *America at the Crossroads*, 2016.

114 Clarence Macartney (d. 1957) waxes eloquent on this text in his famous sermon "Come Before Winter."

115 Henry H. Knight III, *Anticipating Heaven Below*, 2014.

116 Barry L. Callen, *Faithful in the Meantime*, 1997, 2018.

117 Hymn of Isaac Watts, "Our God, Our Help."

118 Dallas Willard, *The Divine Conspiracy*, 1998.

119 George Barna, *America at the Crossroads*, 2016.

120 John Roth, in *Mennonite Quarterly Review*, 1995.

121 In the poem "Bar Time" by Billy Collins, in his *Sailing Alone Around the Room*, 2001.

122 Barry L. Callen, *Caught Between Truths*, 2007.

123 Barry L. Callen, *Golden Nuggets of Truth*, 2024.

124 Richard Rohr, *Yes, And. . . : Daily Meditations*, 2013.

www.ingramcontent.com/pod-product-compliance
Lightning Source LLC
Chambersburg PA
CBHW051750230426
43670CB00012B/2227